Dr Rich Pickins is himself the bestselli...
help books, including *All I Really N*...
the Womb, *If Life is a Bowl of Che*...
Pits?, *Dog Days, Cat Naps — Rel*...
internationally famous diet book *Slim*...

With co-author Norman Puke II, he has boldly ventured into the
unknown with *Was Route 66 A Celestial Highway?*

Founder of the University of Life in Zeroville, Kentucky, Dr Pickins
divides his time between the University and his underwater
condominium off Key Biscayne.

By the same authors

The Bad News Zodiac
The Bad News Horrorscope

Having It All: Success in the Late 20th Century

Edited by Dr RICH PICKINS

GRAFTON BOOKS
A Division of the Collins Publishing Group

LONDON GLASGOW
TORONTO SYDNEY AUCKLAND

For Mary Cecilia Sayers
&
Clare Gibbs, Lucy Apperly and Em Viney

Grafton Books
A Division of the Collins Publishing Group
8 Grafton Street, London W1X 3LA

A Grafton Paperback Original 1989

A CIP catalogue record for this book is available from the British
Library

ISBN 0-586-20535-7

Printed and bound in Great Britain by
Collins, Glasgow

Set in Futura

Contents

Introduction

by Dr Rich Pickins

Hi! I'm Rich Pickins. I believe in success, and the right to succeed. I also believe in quality. That's why I've tracked down the authors of the best and most successful self-help books of our age, and persuaded them to let me distil their works in this single omnibus edition HAVING IT ALL. Never was a book more aptly titled. Digest all these books in my one volume and, as Kipling wrote, you'll be able to 'look triumph and disaster in the eye'. Only, there won't be any disaster.

How could there be? This unique book is a sure-fire winner. It contains priceless advice from such giants of business success as Hetty Zogg and the legendary Mack MacNicknack, not to mention the man with the financial crystal ball, Milt N. Keynes IV. Luminaries from the medical world, such as Dr John B. Sloop and that thrusting go-getter Dale Hendorsen Jnr lend their advice. The spectacularly unconventional and successful Miriam K. Zipper is here, along with world-renowned academic and cultural guru Professor Don Rosenkrantz. From the worlds of style and fashion this book introduces you to Guy Perrière, and reaffirms the revered wisdoms of Grant Calvin and Tex Klein. The world's most famous author, Eugene Flaubert III, unlocks the mysteries of his incredible writing craft, while Marti 'Mr Memory' de Bergi tells you a secret (and how to remember it). Phil O. Facks reports from the Yuppie frontline with his survival tips, while astrological supremo Mike Machola tells you all about finding your 'star' partner. And last — but by no means least — the woman America and the world knows as 'the hostess with the mostest', the amazing Sheri Brillo, reveals extraordinary facts about her very special style of society entertaining.

I want you to enjoy this book. I want you to love it, to treasure it. But most of all, I want you to buy it.

Everyone thinks that Hendon is the tops when it comes to business schools, but one of its most successful alumni doesn't agree. A former astronaut and now a leading restaurateur and mail-order baron, Mack MacNicknack lays it on the line . . .

What They Don't Teach You at Hendon Business School

by Mack MacNicknack

The elite business school at Hendon is admired the world over, and the ivy-covered walls of this famous old Nissen hut located next to the Wavy Line Supermarket off London's prestigious North Orbital Road has been the aspiration of generations of would-be business superstars. Flashing an MBA from this august institution at any multinational will guarantee you an automatic entry into the corporation. Technically proficient though it is, many Hendon graduates are ultimately unsuccessful, and are spotted — not ten years from their graduation day — searching through garbage cans, selling toys on street corners, or peering through your windscreen as they wash and wipe it for a pittance. Why?

Hendon's worldwide reputation rests, primarily, on its ability to teach its pupils vigorous yet fundamentally unimaginative business skills. As a result the alumni graduate into a deceitful world, ill equipped to cope with sleight of hand in international business practice.

Hendonites are taught to think straight in a crooked world, and as a result don't make it. I'm going to teach you how to ride in the executive fast lane without seat belts and *arrive*. It's easy.

Handling the Chairman
I once witnessed a Hendon graduate being introduced to the Chairman of a large multinational on the first day he had joined. Observing the guidelines carefully laid down by Hendon, this

creep repeated the stock phrase, 'I'm delighted to be part of your company, and your world, Sir,' *word for word*. He was immediately fired for sycophancy, and is now working in a circus. Streetwise employees know the smartest thing you can do with Chairmen is to *disregard them completely*, thus emphasizing your native individuality and spirit. Try this method, and tell me I'm wrong.

Tactical Office Location Politics

Hendon says play it straight in office location tactics and the escalator goes right up to the CEO. I say, play it my way and, unorthodox as it may sound, you'll find yourself in the Chairman's seat (if only for a few minutes!). There you are, ensconced in an office in a horrible part of the building. There's no lift, no window and one chair with three legs. The linoleum has run out two floors above, and you're desperate to get at some top level executive shagpile. Well, my solution is brilliantly simple: find out when the Chairman is out to lunch and *move into his office*! It's that simple. In the short time you will enjoy this environment, you can Tipp-Ex out the unflattering references in your personal file and add a nought on to your salary. You'll be discovered, but are likely to survive – even prosper – because you have shown an amazing amount of courage and initiative and the Chairman will be flattered by your attempt to imitate him.

Overseas Travel

The minute you get into overseas travel is the minute you start progressing in my book – and the golden rule in travel is to head for Japan. Unless you're Japanese, no one understands the place, thus allowing you to 'hype' your business meetings in Tokyo to a ludicrous degree. In due course you return and file your report – indicating you're on the brink of pulling off the most brilliant business coup ever – the purchase of Sony and Hitachi for only $747 zillion – but the final 'yes' from Japan may be delayed a little as the intended sale has been referred to a 'committee'. In fact everything in Japan is referred to a committee – including going to the lavatory – so by the time the resounding 'no' has come through three years later, you've left the company and been elected President of IBM on the strength of your Japanese skills. It's that simple.

Furnishing Your Office

Hendon has very clear guidelines on this important issue: frame your MBA certificate and hang it prominently on your office wall, and have no other decorations. I say bull. You've got to make your work environment look individual and different. For starters, why not work out of a king-sized waterbed, and dictate memos to your secretary from a jacuzzi? Purchase a twisted piece of scrap metal, put it on a plinth and name it 'The Closed Market' — a meaningless phrase but one that people will think is important. For pictures, don't even think about framed certificates, but plump for centrefolds from *Penthouse* or *Playgirl* tacked on to your wall, depending on your sex and/or inclination. Whatever your sex it is critically important to smoke a pipe when seeing foreigners in this environment.

Communicating Socially to Achieve Results

I was once at a dinner where an ambitious Hendon graduate was trying to muscle in on the advertising agency for the world's largest manufacturer of in-house detergents. Halfway through my avocado vinaigrette, I heard this man say to the President of the detergent company, 'Who are you?' He didn't get the agency. This only goes to underline an important factor in any business situation: know who you're talking to.

Executive Body Language

Success in dealing with other people is all about reading their body language correctly, and Hendon virtually disregards this science. I have learnt more from body language than a thousand business books! — you can too.

Example: Your secretary says she wants to work late, and at 6.45 walks into your office stark naked, draws the curtains, mixes you a wicked Manhattan, and says she's ready for 'dictation'. If you know body language, you'll know this is her way of telling you the central heating is too high. Move to the thermostat fast.

Or take the process of negotiation. You're trying to shift a consignment of bacon to Israel – but the discount you're offering could be too high – say 40%. The trader you're talking to has his hands round your throat. If you know body language you'll know this is an old Yiddish gesture of affection, and the signs are good for pulling off a big order *at a reduced discount* – say 35%. Go for it.

Or take business introductions. First impressions are vitally important and you have to consider how to maximize your personality-impact potential. Let's take handshakes – it's likely to be the only physical contact you have with a business acquaint-ance, so make the most of it. Grasp the person's hand energeti-cally and maintain contact for *at least* 45 seconds. Then, without letting go and still holding eye contact, kick off your shoes and try humming 'Strangers in the Night'. In doing this you will have established that you are a natural, dominant person and your adversary will be virtually in your pocket.

Location Tactics for Client Entertaining

Generations of Hendon graduates have failed dismally in this critical function of business. It's a minefield.

The Hendon view is the more important the client, the more expensive the restaurant. I say, no. Many times it pays you to take very important clients to very cheap places. I have person-ally dined two Conservative cabinet ministers alfresco in the play area of a Happy Eater. And you know what? These guys loved it *and* came back for seconds! The deal I pulled off was enormous, the bill tiny – which only goes to show how right I was.

Upfront 'Success Secret' Disclosures

People often ask me the secret of my phenomenal success in business. The secret is – and I'm totally open about it – I am an extremely brilliant person.

It's going to be impossible for you to compare your success chart with mine, but if you do have some small measure of success in the world and you are asked for your 'secret', be quite upfront and open about it.

Learning to Love Executive Trinkets

Hendon advises graduates to avoid executive trinkets like the plague, thus creating a sober image. I say, yes, sometimes this is the correct way to go, while other times it pays to invest in one.

For instance, I was lusting for a piece of blue chip action in a major Western stockmarket. I walked into the brokers' meeting wearing a pair of 2-way digital cufflinks, connected to the Dow Jones *by satellite*. Halfway through the meeting I 'beamed in' to the Index. The brokers were impressed. I got my piece of the action.

On another occasion, I was bargaining hard with an eccentric Colombian millionaire for a percentage of the lucrative emerald market. He wouldn't budge. But I had a card up my sleeve: I knew he loved far-out trinkets. Holding eye contact I removed my false teeth in front of him and placed them on my platinum denture caddy! The guy went bananas and I got my percentage.

Up-side Attitude Achievements

Q. What's the best approach to selling? 'Hard' or 'soft'?
A. You can't be dogmatic, and if they teach you at Hendon that it's *always* right to get the jump leads on the gonads in order to make a sale, then they're wrong. That's *usually* the easiest and the best way, but sometimes it pays to be more subtle. Take an example:
   You're trying to shift a consignment of 10,000 Mickey Mouse watches, none of which work. OK, you could threaten your way to a sale, but you'd never sell any of these again, and why lose a valued customer? In my early days, I came across a man with just this predicament. He obtained an exclusive franchise in the first Disneyland and sold each watch for $1, *but with each one, he gave away a $5 bill*! Later, he shot himself but the point is *he made a sale*, and that's what I call an up-side attitude achievement.

Dressing for Business

People often ask me if the Hendon way of dressing for business is the only way. I say, well, let's look at it. Hendon says you should get to the office in a navy pleated skirt, plain tights, sensible shoes, white blouse, single string of pearls, and a Burberry raincoat. And the girls are supposed to dress much the same.

I say – choose to be different. One of the biggest deals I ever closed took place in a nudist colony and, believe me, I didn't let the Hendon uniform get between me and my customer on that occasion! The fact is, you have to get noticed to get on. And if that means turning up to the office on your first day as a partner dressed like Mr Pastry, then I say forget about Hendon and go for it!

Non-Delegation for Power

Another thing that's wrong about the Hendon Way is the question of delegation. Hendon says don't be greedy: be confident of your own power and know when to let go of responsibility in order to achieve more important results yourself. I say, watch out: you wouldn't let your assistant make love to your wife, so why should he do your job? In fact, I not only make love to my wife and do my job, but I also make love to my assistant, type all my own letters, clean the office and polish my secretary's nails as well. This way I feel totally in control of my business environment and ready to face each new challenge. Remember, competition can come from inside the company as well as outside, but if you do all the jobs, you're only competing against yourself. And that's the best competition there is.

The Art of Meetings

Something you're soon going to notice when you get out of Business School and into the real world is that, no matter how efficient you are, the key to getting ahead is getting noticed. Nowhere is this role more applicable than at meetings. Meetings are your great chance to impress senior executives. Don't blow it. Don't shrink into the background. Let's talk it through:

Point 1 Who's going to notice you if you're always on time? Arrive late, maybe through the window, definitely in a Chicago Bears football outfit. No one can ignore this.

Point 2 Everybody likes a nice guy but does he hit the high spots? A favourite game at meetings is who's going to pour the coffee? Executives regard it as a sign of weakness to be the first to 'break' by getting up for the coffee pot, which frequently goes cold as a result. Why not break with tradition? Get up, pick up the coffee, and pour it over the Chairman's head. A temporary setback may ensue, but you will forever be known as the man who bucked the Hendon coffee ceremony.

Executive Preparation for Business Meetings
One of the cardinal rules drummed into the students at Hendon is the old motto, 'Be Prepared'. Sound advice – or is it?

The Hendon Way is prepare yourself for meetings with detailed notes and endless computer stats. All well and good, but isn't this going too far? And hasn't some originality, imagination and flair been taken out of the situation?

I was completely unprepared for one of the most rewarding business meetings of my life. I wanted to break into a Saudi oil cartel, and to do this had to negotiate with a particular Prince of the Royal House of Saud. I arranged a breakfast meeting with this guy at one of my favourite hotels, and ensured the food included Middle Eastern delicacies. Imagine his surprise when the waiter delivered a roasted camel on a forklift truck and set fire to it by our table. Imagine *my* surprise when I discovered the Saudi Prince in question was a vegetarian.

The waiter roared with laughter, and the Prince stormed out of the hotel. I never saw him again, but the story must have got back to the Gulf, as weeks later I was pulled out of my depression by a phone call from his uncle, offering me the exclusive forklift-truck agency for camel catering in a chain of Middle East hotels and their US franchises. Yes, I should have known the Prince was a vegetarian, and no I wasn't properly prepared for my meeting. But in the long term, who's the dummy?

Communicating with Service Staff
I'm the head of a giant corporation, and I come into daily contact with service staff. I'm talking about chauffeurs, masseuses, lift operators and valets. I always make a point of communicating with these people. For instance, my oriental masseuse was giving me a Thai squeeze and pinched a back

muscle painfully — I turned to her and said, 'Watch what the hell you're doing.' How can I forget the occasion when my valet farted while brushing my Savile Row suit? I turned to him and asked him to open the window, adding if he did that again in my presence I would hurl him out of it. On another occasion my chauffeur had the audacity to wish me a 'nice day'. It was raining at the time and my stock had fallen. I was feeling mean. Obviously the guy was hopelessly unobservant. He had to go.

How to Stay at the Top

Unless you're a complete schmuck, you will now have realized four things:

(a) I'm a very important person.
(b) I'm a very successful businessman.
(c) I didn't get to the top by slavishly adopting the Hendon approach.
(d) I'm more important than you are.

But don't despair: you could get further up the ladder by following the rules I've laid down, and if you do get to the top just how are you going to stay there?

Well, I know a thing or two about that, I can tell you. Since the first day I was appointed Chairman, I've always totally disregarded what subordinates have said to me — if they're so smart why aren't they Chairman? — and being a personal friend and fan of Frank Sinatra, I don't mind telling you I've always done it 'My Way'. (Incidentally, I once handled Frankie for a whole season at Caesar's Palace, and renegotiated his contract for very big money indeed — he didn't do so badly out of it either.)

I also learnt at a very early age the benefit of not allowing people to relax around me. For instance, would you believe I was running the X-on Corporation at the age of eight? I was the only guy around wearing short trousers, but if you'd seen the way middle management pandered to my every whim, you wouldn't have believed it. I was big on trifles in those days. I got them. I insisted on a board room table Scaletrix set. I got it. One of the directors beat me at it one day. He got fired. It doesn't do to let anyone feel too close; you've always got to have an edge.

If an employee gets smart with me, I get smart with him — and I can be very smart, like 'the door's over there' smart.

And another thing. Money. Who says it isn't important? It may not be to other people, that's why I don't let them have any, but it is to me. Very important. I've always made sure I'm very very rich, and my employees are very very poor. It pays. Believe me.

So staying on top is largely a matter of keeping everybody else down. I enjoy being top of the pile, I enjoy being the chosen leader, and I enjoy having people under me — it gives me the control I've always wanted out of life. OK, I'm not going to rush off and invade Poland — yet; but I've got my plans for executive *lebensraum*, I can tell you. At Hendon they teach you to play it cool in your quest for executive power. Well, some like it hot and if you can take the heat, get into the kitchen.

For years now the enormous figure of Dr John B. Sloop has been centre-stage in the highest echelons of world medicine — both conventional and alternative. Indeed, he went through the stage on the now famous occasion of his debut speech at the World Diet Conference in 1969. He hasn't looked back since, and after reading this, neither will you.

Eat Fat And Relax To Love Yourself

by Dr John B. Sloop

For years we've been subjected to wall-to-wall fitness and diet books, written by emaciated quacks and weirdos whose own so-called 'wholesome' lives consist of suffering the living death of six pineapples a day, supplemented by pounding the streets of polluted cities wearing silly shorts and shoes and — by the end of the jog — a heavy coating of No. 1 grade urban dog-do.

These crazies cheerily invite pleasure-loving gourmands like you and me to join their anorexic freak-fest. For what? Let me tell you for what: weeks of desperate hardship eyeballing the great Satan of Greed, as you watch your weight plummet from a steady 250 pounds to a stately 247 pounds. Then, late one night, the inevitable happens. The big capitulation: the massive binge — snacking your way through a vast assortment of seriously unhealthy foodstuffs and beverages, you gain 30 pounds within hours, netting off at +27 pounds from where you started. You've gone through what I have dubbed 'The Restriction Cycle', a classic symptom of reversion to form due to mind and body being forced into an unnatural straitjacket after years of self-gratification.

So why bother? I didn't, and it did me no harm. I'm 400 pounds, live in a specially constructed house, and am at peace with myself through my original weight gain, relaxation and self-loving programme — and you couldn't say that of Scarsdale's Dr Tarnower, could you? So follow in my gargantuan footsteps and learn to 'Eat Fat and Relax to Love Yourself'.

The 'Eat Fat' Uncontrolled Calorie Diet

The basics of the uncontrolled calorie diet are perfectly simple: in order to become as enormous as I am you should increase your daily consumption of calories massively. Unless you build up a large reservoir of fat through massive intakes of significantly fatty and cholesterol-ridden foods you will remain an unhappy, deeply dissatisfied and normally sized person.

Let's take someone of 6ft weighing about 170 pounds. This person has an abnormally lean shape and is in my opinion, actually suffering from a medical condition. The rest of the world calls it 'fitness'. I call it stupidity. The individual's diet would look something like this:

Protein   →⎫   Amino acids ⎫
Fats   →⎬ Digestive system → Glucose   ⎬ Body energy
Carbohydrate   →⎭   Fatty acids ⎭

This diet allows the unlucky victim to perform dangerous feats like running on sponsored jogs across deserts, sprint up stairs with ease and participate in violent contact sports. Clearly this abnormality must be corrected. The cure? The Uncontrolled Calorie Diet.

The UCD looks like this:

Digestive → Fats   ⎫   ⎫
System   → Fats   ⎬ Digestive → Fatty acids ⎫ Huge deposits
Panic   → Cholesterol ⎪ system   → Glucose   ⎬ of lard-like
Call for   → Fats   ⎭   → Fatty acids ⎭ body fat

So stuff yourself: there's no mystery to it.

What to Eat for the Uncontrolled Calorie Diet

As a doctor — and as an enormously fat person — I am often asked, 'Doctor, how did you get to be so large?' Those disciples of mine who wish to become seriously overweight and relaxed people who love themselves are always begging me for secret eating tips. Actually it's unbelievably simple: I eat anything I can lay my hands on. The more calories the better. I make no distinction: one day I could consume the contents of my local deli, the next I might go ethnic and make a serious dent in US federal reserves of wienies and bratwurst.

But – and this is vital – you must be consistent in your eating habits. It's no good deciding not to eat to the limit one day, and porking yourself the next. You've got to think huge portions each and every day of your life.

Handling Obesity

Having slavishly followed my uncontrolled calorie diet for a few months, you will be facing the challenge of handling your enormous girth in social situations. The keynote here is to treat people of an average build and weight as total freaks.

Take a typical situation: you're at a cook out. You've just consumed 13 gallons of beer and 85% of the burgers and steaks prepared for the hundred-odd guests. A few tart remarks have come your way – you are (a) a gross pig, (b) welcome no longer.

Immediate action on your part is necessary if you are to carry off the situation with aplomb. Grab a plate. Barge your way to the front of the – by now – famished queue. Pile it high with the remaining food and present it to the host, saying *word for word*, 'looks like *you* have a real malnutrition problem here'. Turn on your heel and depart with as much grace as your juddering 350-pound frame can muster. Easy does, as easy does it.

Relax the Dr John Sloop 'Weigh'

Personally I blame the Ancient Greeks and their Olympiads for originating the fitness and exercising mania that has bedevilled our lives in the late twentieth century. Imagine how much more relaxed and less competitive we'd be today if those maniacs hadn't started it all off by throwing metal plates around and cracking nuts between their buttocks to show how tough they were.

In more recent times I will confess to the odd chuckle or two when I hear of horribly muscular men pulling Pennsylvanian tramcars with their teeth. Turkeys like Atlas could have done with my relaxation programme – and make no mistake. Bodybuilding is a dangerous unhealthy game – grin and you're strangled by your throat muscles. *That's* why 'builders look serious.

Nothing that involves physical effort is good for you – bodybuilding is an extreme example, but are you aware of the incredibly high mortality rate from skipping? Do you know how *many* fatalities there are per annum from the seemingly innocuous activity of sewing? These so-called games and pastimes are, in fact, lethal.

Apart from eating, getting up and going to the lavatory and lying down again, I would counsel strongly against any other form of physical activity. Sex, for instance – and I'm totally delighted to declare it – became a no-go area for me when I topped 320 pounds. I'd been feeling under a lot of pressure to perform, while my partners just felt the pressure.

I banished walking from my life ten years ago. And let me tell you I haven't missed that over-rated activity one iota. My servants hoist me by crane into a specially stretched limo if I want to travel. When I'm being driven 100 yards down the road in New York, I delight in watching deranged bimbos jogging past en route for Central Park.

Loving Yourself

By faithfully following the two clear guidelines I have laid down – gross over-consumption and total relaxation – you will have established a framework from which you will be able to progress with absolute confidence to the biggest prize of all: loving yourself.

Received wisdom, handed down through the aeons, is that man's greatest single characteristic is the ability to love his fellow man. I say bull. First it is necessary to love yourself – very thoroughly. Dr John B. Sloop plc isn't giving *any* loving shares away until the prime stockholder has had his dividend. No, sir!

I've been loving myself for years. I've worked hard at it. I've trained. It wasn't easy at first: the temptation was there, at times, to think of others. But I resisted it.

I can claim, without false modesty, that I had mastered the art of loving myself by the age of ten. As a kid I had rapidly learnt to snack my way through billions of calories at a sitting, and remain virtually immobile all day long, thus creating an ideal relaxed environment. True self-loving *can* be attained at an early age, but only from such pure 'hothousing' conditions, and by the time I had attained double figures I was deeply in love with myself. From that point on, it was only a matter of perfecting the art. OK, I started young — very young — but no age is too old for fundamental change. The potential is there, within each and every one of us, to Eat Fat and Relax to Love Yourself.

When Hetty Zogg first published her phenomenal bestseller, If
I'm So Fantastic, Why Can't I Get A Man?, *she caused a
sensation and changed the lives of millions of women. That this
fantastically successful woman should in reality be so vulnerable
gave hope to millions. It was brave indeed to expose herself in
this way, and I would like to add my thanks for giving me the
right to allow reproduction of her work in this volume. And
talking of reproduction, here's a big thanks to you, Hetty, for
releasing so many women — who might otherwise have been
spinsters — into the sexual arena!*

If I'm So Fantastic, Why Can't I Get A Man?

by Hetty Zogg

If you're into the animal foods business, mail order weight-lifting
equipment and power tools, or even if you just read the finance
pages of your newspaper, you'll have heard of the Hetty Zogg
Corporation. And that's me. From a non-privileged background,
I have conquered discrimination, prejudice and sexism to take
the citadels of success in male-dominated American business.
They may not like me, but in Wall Street now they sure have to
accept me. Until Imelda Marcos had to prune her shopping list, I
was the second-richest woman in the world. Now you don't
need to be a genius to know that I'm numero uno. And I intend
to stay that way. Permanently.

   One night I'd been working late in my suite of offices at the
top of the Zogg Building, tying up the final deals that would give
the Corporation leverage to buy out the government of Brazil —
one of my most celebrated coups. I was feeling on top of the
world, the adrenalin of success pumping through my veins. I
rode the elevator to the atrium, the doorman ushered me to the
waiting limo. And then it hit me. I was going home alone. I had
nobody to share my triumph with. I was forty-two years old,
fantastically successful, with all the trappings that go hand
in hand with immense wealth and immense power. I had

everything that life could offer. Except one thing. I had never been laid.

That night I asked some hard questions. Questions I'd never asked myself. Questions, I now realize, I should have asked years before. In my headlong drive for success — which I still believe is every woman's right (indeed obligation) — I'd missed out on the warmth of human companionship, I'd missed out on the sublime experience of family life. More importantly, I'd missed out on sex. I was forty-two, fantastically successful, and I'd never been boffed.

That night was the first night of my life. I reacted emotionally to this revelation, and after a couple of stiff Manhattans, impulsively I got on the phone and recalled the limo: I didn't want the car. I wanted the driver. Fast.

A few minutes later a uniformed Miles was standing at the door of my penthouse apartment, a perplexed but subservient expression on his face. 'OK, Miles,' I said, 'get that fucking uniform off, and make wild passionate love to me.' I realize now, as I watched his Adam's apple bob up and down, that he was weighing pension rights, company stock options (I like my employees to share in my success), four weeks' paid holiday a year and the swanky uniform tossed in for free, against an order he had no real desire to fulfil. In the end Miles opted for job security, and I remained a virgin. Miles was so scared of me, he couldn't raise a smile, let alone anything else.

I realize now that firing him on the spot was more to do with my problem than his, but in the Zogg Corporation you're either with Hetty or you're nowhere. And whether it was sensitive of me or not, to ask of him what I did ask, you can't escape the fact he wasn't doing his job.

The next day I didn't go to the office. I sat down to do what I have always done when I have a problem: think about it until I've figured out an answer. And when I've got the answer, do something about it. What I thought was this — *if I'm so fantastic, why can't I get a man*? I found that answer, but it was during my months of research into the problem that I realized there were thousands of other women in the same situation. Thousands of women who, in the process of advancement, had sacrificed their sex lives on the high altar of success. I want to share my discoveries with you, to teach you that you can have it all. After putting yourself through the 'I'm So Fantastic ...' Course, I declare that not only will you be an even more successful businesswoman, but you will have the sex life of a hundred Cleopatras, and the pick of a thousand eligible guys. I'm telling you.

The I'm So Fantastic Course

It's easy to say 'I'm so fantastic'. But are you? Before you can establish relationships with other people, the first person you need to know is yourself. Difficult. Or is it? Let's start with the basics. If you are truly sincere about wanting results from this course and making it, you must answer the following questions with absolute honesty — maybe for the first time in your life.

			Score
1. Are you:	(a)	Naturally beautiful?	4
	(b)	OK, but only after creative make up?	3
	(c)	Marginally OK seen in bad light?	2
	(d)	A dog?	1
	(e)	Straight out of the swamp?	0
2. Are you:	(a)	Tall?	4
	(b)	Tall in high heels?	3
	(c)	Boringly average?	2
	(d)	Stumpy?	1
	(e)	Looking for employment in a circus?	0
3. Are you:	(a)	Built like a model?	4
	(b)	Slim?	3
	(c)	Built like a drilling platform?	2
	(d)	Capable of taking the hard ball pitches?	1
	(e)	Absolutely enormous?	0
4. Do you have:	(a)	Huge bazzongas?	4
	(b)	Not what you'd call a mountain range, but a hillock?	3

(c) Dinky dugs? 2
(d) Nothing? 1
(e) A surplus of male hormones? 0

5. Do you have an ass that:
(a) Construction workers whistle at when you walk down the street? 4
(b) You would like construction workers to whistle at when you walk down the street? 3
(c) Construction workers wouldn't dive off buildings to get at? 2
(d) Construction workers would whistle at in sheer amazement if you could ever get your mountainous bulk down the street? 1
(e) Construction workers would feel embarrassed around? 0

6. You meet a good-looking guy. Do you:
(a) Engage him in conversation, before asking him for a date? 4
(b) Flash your goodies at him? 3
(c) Rest your hand on his thigh? 2
(d) Hide under the table? 1
(e) Call the police? 0

7. How many serious boyfriends have you had?
(a) None. 0
(b) None. 0
(c) None. 0
(d) None. 0
(e) None. 0

If you're sure you've answered all these questions honestly, add up your score and check it against the character analysis below.

24–20 I think that women like you give the rest of us a bad name by buying books like this, just so you can laugh at those less fortunate than yourself. So goodbye. Forever.

* * *

19–16 You have the potential to go all the way in life, but lack the self-confidence. Which of your parents let you down so badly? You must conquer these feelings of inadequacy to progress.

15–11 OK, little Miss Average. You want to remain a wallflower forever, that's fine, but don't expect to make it with the guys unless you work hard at the lessons in this book. Nobody is saying it's going to be easy with this kind of score.

10–6 This is approaching the twilight zone. You are very unattractive to men, but you have a big character and are able to face up to the reality of your looks. Given a certain amount of surgery, you are the kind of challenge I've always enjoyed, and just the type of woman this book is written for.

5–1 Short of a head transplant, there is little that I can do for you, but the fact that you have bought this book stands as testimony to some glimmer of self-respect in you that maybe we could work into something attractive to a male—not necessarily human—creature.

0 I'll refund the cost of this book. Go back to munching ferns on all fours.

So. You have the score. You have your character analysis. Good news for some, not so good for others. I think we're taking the 1–5s out of it at this stage, but certainly from 6 upwards you're in there with a fighting chance of getting that man, and having that sex. So, the first exercise that I want you to carry out in the 'I'm So Fantastic' Course is to admit to yourself what you are, and then go up to a man – any man – and tell him about it. (Men like candidness from women. They like to feel close to a woman's problems – even big problems like yours.) In doing this you will no longer be a prisoner of your own inadequacies. So step on it: get out there and find a man!

Where To Meet Guys

So. You've decided to take some action. Get a little dating in. The first thing you're going to need — and if you didn't know this already things are worse than they really should be for a mature lady — the first thing you're going to need is a guy. Where are you going to find one? Where are the red-blooded men in this country? Believe me, they're everywhere. There are men at ball games, department stores, fast-food restaurants and libraries. There are men on street corners, there are men in jail (hard to get to, I know, but they're there). There are even men on the moon! If a girl wants to find one, and I mean *really* wants to find one, then she can. It's simply a matter of confidence.

Your Opening Shot

So. You've found where the guys hang around. Now you move to your 'Opening Shot'. It couldn't be more critical. You can blow lots of things in life, but if you blow this you're in trouble. Don't panic when you're introduced, or introduce yourself, to some guy. Take the initiative. I've examined this procedure intensively, and the surefire winners listed below have never let me down.

1. 'Is that your real nose, or are you just pleased to see me?'
2. 'Show me your kennel, showdog.'
3. 'I love the way your eyebrows meet in the middle.'
4. 'This will surprise you, but I'm a virgin.'
5. 'Only a man like you would be daring enough to wear flares.'

How To Make a Man Commit

OK — so you've found a nice guy — or guy, at least — and you've been on a few dates, maybe even boffed around a little (if you have, incidentally, you've just blown the best way to make him commit, but never mind, there are other ways), and now you want to settle down with him and — let's not beat around the bush here, girls — you want to get married and start a family. How are you going to pin the guy down? The first thing to remember is that you're on your own here. A guy may want to go on a date, but no way is he going to want to get married, particularly to you.

So here's what you do.

Method 1. As mentioned above, if you've been careful you haven't given in to his carnal desires. Simply hold out for the wedding. After all, you've held out for your whole life up to now, so you're probably pretty used to it.

Danger: the guy will simply dump you and find some other girl who'll give him what he wants. This is a double disaster for you, as you haven't even got laid in the process. You may prefer:

Method 2. Boff him into submission. Just get hold of the guy, and give him so much sex that he has to marry you to feed his addiction to the act of love.

Method 3. Tell him you're pregnant. *Danger*: the usual.

Method 4. Beg him on bended knees. This is not exactly the approved way to go for a successful businesswoman, but I won't tell if you don't.

Method 5. Home cooking. They do say the way to a man's heart is through his stomach via his uglies, and I say there's nothing wrong with a few traditional values occasionally.

Method 6. Be really strong. Tell him he's going to marry you, and he's one lucky jerk. Get him down to that church so fast, his feet don't touch the ground.

Danger: you're going to end up marrying this wimp.

Getting To Know Men

The first rule of war is: know your enemy. In this case, men. Believe me, ladies, men are your enemy. I've discovered this in the business world, like thousands of other women before me. And it's true in the pursuit of partnership and sexual fulfilment as well. Men don't want relationships with women like us. We have to *make* them want us, and to do that you've got to know what you're up against.

So what is a man? I've often heard it said that a man wants only one thing. Well, in my experience, that's just not true. In short order wants beer, pizza, a ball game on TV every night, a Corvette Stingray, a massive penis, a machine pistol and a sex slave. You're going to have to handle this guy very carefully, if you're going to get what you want from him. Here are some tips:

Why Should I Be Ashamed Of Success?

OK. At work you're a creative and powerful businesswoman. When you say jump, senior vice-presidents ask how far. When you say lunch, you're talking your usual table at Sardi's. When *Time* magazine says success, they mean you. But somehow, the minute you walk into a singles bar, or get put next to a man at a dinner party, you're completely at a loss for anything to say. The man is probably just the kind of low-grade executive under-achiever you chew out before breakfast each day at the office. Yet suddenly, you find yourself simpering in front of this guy's moronic conversation about cars and football — and actually feeling ashamed of your own success, compared with his pathetic lack of it. Stand up to men, I say. Stand up to the bastards. Always carry a bank statement and your last paycheck. Whack them down and ask if anyone in the room can beat them. If they can't — you win. They take off their clothes.

Taking Out the Competition

A good man is hard to find, and often even harder to keep. So, once you've landed your fish, how are you going to take out the competition from waves of kamikaze women desperate to bump your hunk's uglies, or die in the attempt?

Your man will appreciate your desire to keep the competition at bay. Men love to be fought over. Challenging your prime rival to a bout of naked mud wrestling is the type of challenge that appeals to men — he'll probably ask some friends around to watch the show — but does it appeal to you? Supposing you lose, leaving you lying in the mud watching your man walk away with your rival! In my view it's smarter to take out the opposition at an early stage, before competition for your man is even formalized. You can mace them if they say hello to him. You can tamper with their brakes if they get frisky. You can blackmail them, or simply blow them away.

* * *

So. That's the 'I'm So Fantastic' Course. It is fantastic, isn't it? If you adopt all of the rules and guidelines laid down, you can be a successful woman and be screwing your brains out each and every goddam' day of your life with the man (or men) of your choice.

I was a virgin up to the age of forty-two. The only thing I'd ever laid was a table. Now I'm slightly older than that, with a fabulous husb, three fabulous kids, and Grigor, my extra fabulous eighteen-year-old toy boy hunk, who I keep in the gilded cage of a mid-town apartment.

Believe me, every word of my story is true. I've been there. I've done it, and now I'm telling you to get out there and do it as well. And in doing so you need never have to say again, 'If I'm So Fantastic, Why Can't I Get A Man?'

Grant Calvin and Tex Klein have been friends of mine for more years than I care to remember. Their sharp analysis of the relationship between dress sense and business sense has been invaluable to my own success, and it will be to yours as well.

Dress For Success
by Calvin & Klein

In the late twentieth century ambition and image go hand in hand. Not since the days of the Medicis in the fifteenth century has power been so inextricably linked with style and fashion. Ambitious people must have the right image to get on. An image which transmits those *crucial* success signals.

As leading consultants in the world of fashion and image we have, time and time again, seen people with all the right qualifications, but all the wrong clothes, gunned down when it comes to the key positions, the key jobs.

In this book we've talked to some real winners — and a few losers — at the white-hot interface of fashion and style in today's business world. Each has his or her story to tell. The success stories are obvious and so, unfortunately, are the failures.

But the message always seems to be the same: it's no longer enough to think that Brooks Brothers or Saks Fifth Avenue are going to be able to carry you through in your drive to success. This is the era of the individual and the entrepreneur; the world of the person who stands out from the crowd. Take some of the tips from our case studies, but don't slavishly follow them — that wouldn't be individual. Find a style and identity of your own. By absorbing these experiences, you too can learn how it's done.

The first phenomenon we looked at was the rise, rise and rise of Spandex . . .

Making it with Spandex
Today many of the world's bright achievers are realizing the benefits of professional Spandex clothes. 'They're light, attractive

and I just love the sheen,' says Carol Dix, a Wall Street foreign exchange dealer. 'The accent's on comfort and conformity for me,' remarks Bunty Staggles, a blue chip commodity broker in the City of London, relaxing in his dark Spandex suit with gold pinstriping. 'I can splint in them,' says Nori Shinbashi, a young dealer in a hurry on Tokyo's Stock Exchange, who loves Spandex for the ease of mobility it gives him as he rushes across the trading floor.

Spandex as leisurewear has, of course, been around since medieval times — references to it being found in *Beowulf* and *Les Très Riches Heures du Duc de Berry* — but it is only in the late twentieth century that it has really caught on for the professional man or woman.

'Sales are expanding like wildfire,' declares Wayne Dworkin, head of consumer marketing at Glit Ron the leading spandex company worldwide, 'particularly in the financial sector. Do you know, Citicorp and Chase now insist their bank managers wear three-piece spandex suits?'

Visit any store these days and you'll find an exciting selection to choose from.

Steve Terrazzo, chief buyer (menswear) at Macys, says: 'We can't get enough spandex to keep up with demand. I've seen so-called "civilized" Wall Street bankers fighting like animals to get their hands on a pair of Spandex crotchless underpants. It's incredible.'

Izzi Banzai, at Tokyo's top department store Zero, Zero confirms this: 'We got whole container ship roaded with Splandex. Japan go Splandex clazy.'

The success story continues round the globe, penetrating even Third World markets. Sierra Leone's Finance Minister Ju Ju Bafodia had to clamp down on Spandex sales, when the government discovered 40% of the g.n.p. was being spent on imports for the material. (Spandex is, in fact, totally unsuitable for the tropics, which makes the national craze even more incredible.) Inevitably, some Third World politicians suspect a Western conspiracy to further impoverish their economies with massive Spandex imports — a suspicion that Wayne Dworkin of Glit Ron is anxious to quash: 'At the end of the day, it's just a phenomenally successful material. There's no substance in the conspiracy theory.'

From a great product, to a great commercial style concept, and one of the pioneers of the Dress For Success philosophy, let's move on to . . .

Pro-Ballerina Security

Ronnie Mailorder started his first security service in the late Sixties. 'I made mistakes with that company,' says Ronnie, interviewed relaxing in his Fresno condo. 'I was naïve enough to believe a security service should be conventional – squads of big hairy guys with bad-boy sideboards, blue crimplene trousers and fake badges. Dodge vans with grills. Business ticked over, but we weren't in the big league. I knew we had to do something different – really different – to attract new customers. One night, early '76, I was watching some ballet on TV and hit on this great idea. Why not have my men dress up like ballet dancers? It would get us noticed and no criminal is going to stage a robbery on security men dressed in tights and tutus. It had to be good for business.

'My guys were all heteros and I had trouble persuading them, particularly as I insisted on a female chorus line. Believe me, they went along with the idea when I hiked their wages, and threw in the gear for free.

'The company's name was changed to Federal American Interstate anti-Robbery Investment Empire Security – F.A.I.R.I.E.S. – I thought it was appropriate – and I hyped *the* new concept in security to the media. Our first job delivering cash to a Bank of America was heavily attended by TV and Press, and there wasn't a dry eye around as my boys skipped out of the van to a piece from *Swan Lake*, tippytoed to the bank and opened the hatch. Easy!'

Chuckling, Ronnie sits back and dips his paw into the bowl of brightly coloured jellybeans that is his permanent companion, a bowl fashioned from an olde-style security helmet. 'From there on in we never looked back,' recalls Ronnie. 'Now we've got F.A.I.R.I.E.S. in every country in the world, including special modern dance sections to service trendy new hi-tech industries.

They've even asked us to service till-receipts at Sadlers Wells and handle the Ballet Rambert's wage deliveries, for Chrissakes! Might just do it, too!' exclaims Ronnie, throwing back his head and bellowing with laughter — exposing over 2lbs of masticated jellybeans.

Ronnie Mailorder turned his business around with a great concept — but essentially, he didn't change the nature of his business or his staff.

Let's look at someone who did. Ted Sanchez first had to transform himself, before he could become a major force in the business world. But before he tells his uniquely personal story, let's look briefly at the historical background of what he's talking about.

What Colour Is your Warpaint?

From earliest times, people have dressed for war. Not just in armour-plating, but also in ritual colours, with significant designs and symbols — even, in the case of ancient Britons, with blue woad and nothing else. Like medieval soldiers, soccer players today identify each other by their uniforms, and their supporters march under banners. And, like ancient Britons, American footballers wear stripes of face-paint beneath their eyes. What's the moral of the story for today's businessman or businesswoman? The moral is this: business is war, and if you dress for business, you dress for war.

Ted Sanchez is a senior VP at the major New York public relations consultancy, Smitt, Smitt and Schitt. Sitting in the unrestrained elegance of his 99th-floor penthouse executive office suite, Ted is the first to admit that his career was going nowhere before he understood the meaning of ritual and colour in the world of business appearances.

'Sure,' he says, 'I was a no-good telephone salesman selling no-good space in a dumb-fuck magazine. I was wearing a blue pinstripe three-piece suit, a button-down shirt and a club-style tie, and that's not all! Would you believe I was wearing Old Spice aftershave as well? Did I say going nowhere? Make that going backwards!'

So what turned it around for Teddie Sanchez? Let him pick up the story.

'I'm sitting on the phone one day trying to sell some dummy an ad in the magazine when I forget about the job and just start, like, talking with the guy. Turns out he's a history professor at some college and he majors in ancient warfare. The dude tells me about these guys taking off all their clothes and painting themselves with blue woad and slaughtering Romans and people. As I listened I began to feel a special affinity with them.'

Sanchez fingers an old flint arrow-head as he speaks — excitedly now — of this turning point in his life.

'I started to study those guys — the ancient Brits like Boadicea and the legendary Hannibal, the man who led huge armies of elephants to Rome. I thought, "Hey, these are my kind of guys — these are leaders." I thought, "This isn't so far removed from business today in the Big Apple." In their day, the Romans had all the civilization that was going, and these Goths wanted a piece of it. So they marched in, and they took it. In our day, J. Walter Thompson has all the public relations business in town and other agencies want a share of the market. So it's war.'

So what did Ted Sanchez, telephone salesman, *do* about all this? Calmly now, he takes the arrow-head flint and puts it back in the human skull from which, in his excitement, he had removed it.

'What did I do? I'll tell you what I did. One weekend I made myself an axe. Then on Monday morning I took off all my clothes, covered myself in blue poster paint and came into work. No motherfucker was going to give *me* any hassle on the subway, man!

'Between the subway station and the office, I had my first — and really my only — setback. It rained, and the paint disappeared. But when I got to work, the magic power of the stuff still seemed to weave its spell. If anyone laughed, or in any way implied that I was out of line, I hit them with the axe, and I hit them hard.'

So what happened then?

'Well, things moved kinda quickly after that. I was taken off the telephones after I axed my supervisor and I was put in charge of customer relations. I wore water-resistant woad. I began to develop my own team of executives. People who were loyal to me as well as the company. I killed a lot of people who refused to swear an oath of allegiance and dress the same way as me. I became the youngest-ever senior v.p. in the company listing and I'm very proud of that. I also believe I have played a significant role in expanding this agency's share of the market to its current pole position. We are now the biggest killing company in America and on any given day, we can field an army of approximately fifteen thousand naked axemen. In effect, we control the city from about 73rd to maybe 141st Street.'

That's not bad in the business battlezone that is New York City today. Not bad at all. But it was with some relief that we left the Schitt building, and made our way to our next interviewee, and a totally different 'dress' concept.

Wake Up To Make Up

Mike Porco's office is the office of any highly successful red-blooded American male. There are his certificates on the wall, there's the baseball signed by Joe Namath, and there's the enlarged photograph of his genitals proudly displayed above the door lintel.

It's all the more surprising, then, to discover that Porco's phenomenal rise in corporate America is entirely due to the fact that he wears women's make-up. Period. Let Mike tell his extraordinary story, and how he came to use cosmetics in the first place.

'First I used eye shadow and Compact II. It just seemed the natural thing to do', says Mike, recalling the eventful day when he 'took the plunge'.

'I was a fledgling director of the Poubelle Corporation back then (1974), and I'd got the strong impression that ... I wasn't making an impression where it counted – right at the top. The President of Poubelle used to look straight through me. I knew I had to go out of my way to be noticed and the best way of achieving this – and improving my looks – was through make-up. I remember the situation well: it was at a board meeting, and I wanted to tie up an exclusive agency in the Far East. It was a heavy move for Poubelle and the board was nervous. Very nervous. I slipped out of the room and applied a generous amount of eye shadow and Compact II. No one noticed the difference until I leapt to my feet and cried at the top of my voice "Let's give it to the South Koreans."'

Mike toys with an oversize roll-ball deodorant as he talks about that decisive moment in his career.

'There was a long silence. The President finally broke it by saying – "Mike's right. This must be the way to go." As it turned out Seoul didn't have a clue how to handle the agency, but by then it didn't matter. I'd made it big – very big – at Poubelle, and transferred to a rival corporation who paid me a big, big salary and a big, big executive make up allowance.'

Despite the silly name, Mike Porco made it into the league of major players. As he candidly says, 'I like to believe my success was in no small part due to my insistence on *looking and being different*.' Wake up to make up, guys!

It seems only natural to turn, at this stage, from a man who wears make-up, to a woman who reversed the principle as successfully as Porco . . .

Dressing for Sex-Image Juggling

For eight years Marilyn Foxman worked as a systems analyst in a large computer company. As she freely admits, her career was going nowhere. Marilyn: 'Things weren't gelling for me. I was getting lost in the corporate crowd. By the time I was 28 I realized I had to do something different to succeed. I decided to roughen up my image.' Image?

'I quit shaving my legs and armpits. I took to wearing heavy tweed suits and hobnailed boots to the office. And I smoked a pipe. For a while I wore a monocle, and the only headgear I would countenance was a Sam Spade-style trilby.

'Gradually things started to move,' reflects Marilyn, now the Vice-President of the self-same computer company. 'I'd be asked to the odd weekend game of baseball or golf. The odd jocks party. I realized things were really happening when the guys in the office started to wear heavy tweed suits and old-fashioned hats — obviously they were threatened by me, and wanted to compete.

I felt good about that. Soon it was *de rigueur* for aspiring young males in the company to wear these curious clothes and smoke pipes. Naturally at this stage, I switched back to the feminine look, making them look like weirdo turkeys, and me like the only sane person in the company. Within two years I'd made it to VP'

No one can deny that Marilyn Foxman has made it, and made it in her own unorthodox and highly original way. And if Marilyn strikes you as coming from way out on the left field, you'll be amazed at our next interviewee . . .

Bookwear

Gloria Shafto is an unashamed book freak. 'I read all the time,' says Shafto, now senior commissioning editor at a major publishing house, 'and since I was always caught short for reading material I figured why not wear my favourite literature?' So declares this literary virago, relaxing in a skyvitex-bound edition of *The Red Badge of Courage*.

'My first attempt at bookwear was toting a copy of *Little Dorrit* on my head — it was raining that day. Later I went jogging wearing only *The Seven Pillars of Wisdom* taped across my chest, and two copies of *The Well of Loneliness* for pantyhose. I remember someone at the office suggested it should have been *The Two Pillars of Wisdom*,' recalls Gloria (36–22–36), 'but what the hell would T. E. Lawrence have made of that? Or Radclyffe Hall for that matter?' reflects this buxom woman of letters with a laugh.

At weekends Gloria went swimming looking more than alive in a copy of Gogol's *Dead Souls*, and frequented beach parties in a drip-dry edition of *Leaves of Grass* — one of her favourites.

'Sooner or later it had to catch on at work,' says Gloria. 'After all, we were all in the same game together — books. I knew it was really working, when the President wore a copy of Audubon's *Birds of America* — OK, it is physically the largest book published in the US, but I put this down to his shyness.'

Pretty soon the whole company was like a bookshop with

mobile displays, and the sales department extended the idea and instructed the reps to wear the Fall and Spring lists. Since it went over to an official Bookwearing policy, Gloria's company has trebled its turnover, and competing publishing houses are rushing their sales forces into Bookwear. 'It worked for me, and it worked for the company. Why don't you try it?' says a sublimely self-confident Ms Shafto.

Despite the success stories there isn't a crock of gold at the end of every rainbow, certainly not for Tony Zero . . .

Coping with Hair Loss to Dress Bald

Tony Zero lost his hair one night. 'It was traumatic,' recalls Tony, now a door-to-door wet fish salesman in Kentucky. 'I woke up one morning, stumbled into the bathroom, stared in the mirror and thought, "It's Yul Brynner!" I didn't recognize myself.'

Tony lost his hair to executive stress. Medical experts now reckon on tens of thousands of young men and women losing their hair overnight — every night. Pressure, office and urban life take their toll on them. Traumatic? You can say that again. Tony: 'I wouldn't go near the office until I'd got a wig. I was fixed up quickly with a Wonder Weave and returned to work, but it fell off one day when I was polishing the President's shoes and the game was up. I had to go!'

A tragic story, but while Tony couldn't cope with baldness, others can. Take Mike Tachiolo, now President of the ShowDogg Corporation.

'Yep, it happened to me. I was 32 and inching my way up the corporate ladder. They'd put some carpet down in my office at last and given me a desk with four legs. I was trying hard to make an impression, but wasn't succeeding,' reflects Mike, 'people found me dull and lacklustre, and I guess the pressure was showing. I went home one night and woke up next morning with 100% hair loss. I was competely bald. I remember saying to myself, "Mike, you get back to work right now or you get out of the corporate game forever." You know what I did? I ran down Fifth Avenue stark naked straight into the office. They started to notice me then at ShowDogg's, let me tell you,' says Mike with a smirk.

Mike made a virtue of his baldness. He made it *work* for him. In the hothouse, competitive atmosphere of ShowDogg, his frank approach to 100% hair loss – and occasional office nudity – helped him win friends. 'A lot of people were behind me,' he recalls. Pretty soon he was vaulting up the corporate ladder and made it to President by 38.

So Tony Zero lost out, while Mike Tachiolo won through. And you know why? Because at the end of the day Mike had the balls to use his deficiency positively and Tony didn't. It's as simple as that.

Many people are now recognizing that shoes are a vital indicator of a person's character. Let Lee Limox expand on this . . .

Winning with Tactical Footwear

'I love white shoes,' declares Lee Limox, 'preferably very long and pointy.'

In the past Lee wore Bass Weejun loafers and Brooks Brothers suits. 'Those were my button-down days,' he recalls. 'It was a bad period for me – my image was hopelessly confused. And when your image is in a mess, it reflects on your inner being.'

Lee is now a prosperous realtor and owner of a chain of laundromats in Hoboken. So what changed? Lee: 'By wearing eye-catching clothes, I started to make an impression on business associates. I majored on shoes – they just got more and more way out. Things started to go well for me, and I figured my success was related to my footwear. My shoes became a talking point. I'd be trying to close a deal, and it was weird – people would be hypnotized by the 4ft-long pair of medievals, or my diamanté snakeskin disco boots with eleven-inch stacks and glitter inlays. They just weren't concentrating at all. I had guys signing away acres of real estate – in prime locations – for peanuts.'

Success has brought Lee many rewards, and as he relaxes in his penthouse wearing an old pair of L. L. Bean bootees with the now-dated digital calculator ankle-pads, we'll leave him with the final word: 'I believe passionately in footwear. It pays, believe me.'

But what of the older generation? Let Nat Peabody tell his extraordinary story...

Dressing for Seniors' Success

Nat Peabody is known across the world as the man who pioneered the concept of dressing for Seniors' Success, and his bestselling book, *Dress Young, Die Old*, is treated like a bible by millions of Grey Panthers.

Nat was the longest-serving sales executive at the Arthur Sweetly Gentleman's Suit Emporium in Streatham, London, when he reached retirement age in 1981. 'I was 65,' says Nat, 'but I didn't feel like retiring. I had been wearing the same suit and measuring inside legs for nearly fifty years, and I thought experience like that had to count for something. You had a feel for the job. But Sweetly's just wanted to throw me on the scrap heap. So I took my pension and set up shop across the road as a clothing consultant. Boy! Was I in for a hard time! In the first year of business, my wife Marge and I received only two commissions – one from an undertaker who wanted to make his image a little more conservative, and one from a young man who wanted to wear Marge's underwear! We were flat bust inside 12 months.'

Nat looks visibly shaken at this point, as if the memory of these dark days is still very hard to bear. Worse was to follow the collapse of the clothing consultancy, as Nat's bestselling autobiography, *Suits Me*, told in such stark detail. Marge never recovered from her sense of failure and Nat was soon measuring her up, not for a new dress but a wooden box.

'Well,' says Nat, 'that was the hardest time, but looking back it was the making of me. I asked myself some hard questions about what went wrong with the consultancy, and came to some tough conclusions.

'I had been wearing the same worsted sta-prest Arthur Sweetly suit since I left school. I was – and I didn't mind admitting it – a boring dresser.

'What young person would ever have wanted to dress like me? And if a young person, with love, life and success ahead of him didn't want to dress like me, why should an old one?

'So I decided to change my luck with a change of image. I went up to the loft and designed my own range of sequined leather disco wear. And I wore it. I manufactured a complete wardrobe in see-through taffeta. People loved it.

'Word soon spread. Stars like Brian Ferry and Julio Yglesias were beating a path to my door. Marillion and John Denver wanted to sign me on an exclusive retainer. That was all very well — but I was interested in people even older than that.

'I thought: "If I can be this successful, why can't others of my age? Why should we look like boring old fogeys with nothing left to offer when a splash of pink satin could turn us into big players in the game of life?" So I founded "Grancare".'

Nat's infectious enthusiasm makes it all sound simple now, but building up 'Grancare' from a single shop in Tooting to a multinational conglomerate quoted on Wall Street inside five years must have taken some doing. What is Nat's real secret of success?

'I give a lot of credit to my boxer shorts,' says Nat, with a smile that seems to say he isn't joking. 'For years, old people have worn boring old long johns. They sap your vitality. You've got to dress young if you're going to act young, and my Batman Boxers simply keep me going.'

Thanks to just one man, the Grancare Company now employs more than 10,000 people over 65, and old people designer clothes have become big business.

You'd have to be extremely dumb if you hadn't guessed by now that how you dress is the key to getting on in life. Everybody needs clothes at one time or another — even Mike Tachiolo! — and the message from the new leaders in our business life is 'Dress For Success'. Get out there, and do it.

What can you say about Miriam K. Zipper? The sheer originality and brilliance of her thinking has left a whole generation breathless with admiration. She is singlehandedly responsible for the whole Reward-Punishment concept, which now plays such a major part in our corporate and daily lives. Miriam is a unique person, with a unique philosophy . . .

Celebrity Reward-Punishment Weekends

by Miriam K. Zipper

ESP and EST were big box office in the Sixties and early Seventies. Times change. Values change. Attitudes change. By the mid-Seventies I realized a bold new concept was required to cater for highly successful men and women who needed a quick hike out of the fast lane.

My theory was simple. Big achievers are under big pressure. They don't have time for intercourse. Let me rephrase that: they've always got time for intercourse, but the mental variety? Forget it. So I said to myself, OK, these so-called successful people are, essentially lonely and confused. They'd got lost in the corridors of power, and they'd forgotten how to relate. To themselves, and to others. So I figured why not establish a weekend retreat where the dynamic, the successful and the celebrated could challenge themselves in unusual circumstances, could come and re-learn that most human of instincts: the instinct to relate? Out of this simple idea was born the Reward-Punishment ™ philosophy, and eventually, after several years of hardship and intellectual refinement, the Celebrity Reward-Punishment Program™, and the whole Reward-Punishment ™ movement. Little did my husband Rudolpho and I think of *that* at the time though. Let me go back to the beginning for a moment.

We were living in a trailer park on a land-fill site called San Andreas City, and believe me we didn't have enough cents to watch pay-TV, even if we'd had a TV. Now, we own the whole Reward-Punishment ™ Channel, rated No. 8 across the nation in advertising revenue, and the enormous Zipper Complex, our Ranch in New Mexico which is home to thousands of celebrities and ordinary Americans every year.

So what exactly is the Reward-Punishment™ philosophy? Basically, it hasn't changed since the day I first dreamed it up. I was sitting in the trailer park watching our eldest son, Ramon, playing ball with his father. The kid just didn't seem able to hit the hard-ball pitches coming at him from Rudolpho. Rudolpho had tried just about everything to show him how to swing the bat, but the kid wasn't learning. So — and I'm just sitting on the steps of the trailer drinking a can of lite beer (I'd been saving for weeks) and watching my husband and my son, thinking about nothing in particular — when Rudolpho snatches the bat from Ramon and hits him with it, really hard. Then he hands back the bat, and Ramon connects with the very next pitch. Rudolpho is so happy, he reaches into his pocket and gives the boy our last fifty cents! And suddenly it comes to me: *Punishment* and *Reward*. It's the most basic human motivation, and if that's true, then it can be applied to the most basic human need, which as I've already said, is the need to relate. *That* was the beginning of my philosophy. What made it the success it has become — and Reward-Punishment™ is probably the most successful philosophy of all time in terms of earnings-per-share and profit-to-sales ratios — was, I truly believe, another idea of Rudolpho's. He said OK, you've got something here that literally *everyone* needs, everyone, that is, who isn't a bum or a Communist, so who are we going to go to first? Why not start with the people who need it most, the people under the most pressure, the people who are so famous that they are totally removed from other people and therefore have the hardest time relating: in other words, celebrities. And sure enough we began to get celebrities, and as the celebrities began to get results the other people came too. In the Fall of '78 I held my first Celebrity Reward-Punishment Weekend™ (CRPW) in a parking lot outside a shopping mall. The celebrity guests — we didn't ask them to pay unless they were totally satisfied — were Burt Bacharach, Spiro T. Agnew and Joan Crawford. I'm happy to say the weekend was a success.

The business prospered. In the summer of '79 we bought an extensive plot of land and village of adobe huts in New Mexico, which grew into the fabulous Zipper Complex. Word was now getting round the celebrity circuit that the Zipper was the place to be when the going got tough. As it expanded the public were allowed access to what we had to offer. But hey, enough of my yackin', let's take a look at a typical weekend. The kind of weekend that *you* are just a toll-free call and credit card authorization away from.

Friday evening you leave the office in, say, New York City, and four hours later you could be touching down in Tucson, Arizona. That's just the kind of executive mistake the weekends are designed to eliminate, since the nearest airport to the Zipper is 400 miles to the north-east at Albuquerque. So, let's say you finally get in on Saturday morning. What would you expect to find?

The CRPW™ will already be in full swing as you check into the beautifully appointed Evita Peron Ramada Inn at the heart of the Zipper Complex. On this particular Saturday let's look in on one of our regulars, General Pinochet, and see what he's getting out of the weekend. The first thing you may think, as one of our ever-helpful Zipper boys totes your bags to your suite, is why on earth should Chile's world-famous no-nonsense super bad-assed dictator need a morale and confidence boosting weekend like this, and second what is he doing being escorted on to the freeway driving a 5 mph golf-kart dressed in a lime-green tutu?

I'll tell you, because sometimes it does need spelling out. We've all got problems, and even the toughest people are no exception. The General has faced up to this. He is a military man, a man of great pride; but he is also a man who finds it difficult to relate to others. In order to unlock the full potential of his warm personality, we knew we had to get beyond that stiff macho image. This is where the punishment part of the weekend comes in. After an hour on the freeway suffering the abuse of a thousand truckers, rednecks and other gun-lobby activists the General is pretty much ready to open his mind to anything, provided he can get off the freeway alive. Safely back at the

Zipper, Pinochet has one more task before he gets down to the reward of an afternoon's target practice on the small arms range: he has to shake hands with six Communist dissidents who escaped Chile with the help of Amnesty International. Sadly for our plucky helpers — not really Communists at all but part-time Zipper employees from the Wabash County Kiwanis — the General suddenly produced an Uzi submachine gun, with which he blew them away. 'Naughty, General, naughty,' I said. 'One more move like that and you're 'gator bait.' The General was transported back on to the freeway, this time on a 2 mph milk float, and the whole process began again, until he learnt how to relate.

I don't need to tell you President Botha of South Africa has his problems. Repressing 90% of his population looms large in the President's mind, so large he needed time out to relax and relate with us at the Zipper. The Prez. arrived late Friday night, and since it'd been a long flight I figured the guy deserved a reward, so he spent Saturday morning and afternoon relaxing in a hot tub watching linked *Miami Vice* episodes. But being the man he is I also figured he deserved a choice punishment. Six o'clock he got the call. Could he get into the waiter's uniform provided and be at the El Paradisio Restaurant 6.45 sharp? He didn't like it, but showed up. I said, 'P.W., we've got a party tonight and it's your privilege to serve the guests.' '*Serve* them?' he quavered. 'Too right, you funky bastard,' I said. 'Meet the Memphis Tabernacle Choir.'

Serving 600 black gospel singers singlehanded at table doesn't come easily to the President of South Africa, but I'll say something for that man, he went at it with all the stolid determination of a Voortrekker. P.W.'s nerve finally broke when they went for him with their dessert forks, and we found him hiding in the deep freeze. I figured he'd already had enough punishment for the weekend, and he'd absorbed a whole lot about relating to other people in a very real way, so come Sunday we let him out on to the golf course, before exiting for the SAA 747 warming up on the tarmac at Albuquerque.

Heavy-duty baddies are no longer flavour of the month in Eastern Europe, which is a crying shame. I've often thought what

47

fun we'd have had with Lavrenti Beria and Uncle Joe Stalin. But General Jaruzelski came to us once.

Looking at General J. on the news — greeting Soviet bigwigs at Warsaw airport, going walkabout in Cracow — you could think the man is a little stiff and unbending. But if you think that now, I can't tell you what he was like the first time he checked into the Zipper. Solidarity were all the rage, and to say the General was uptight would be an understatement of seismic proportions. He kept raving about Gdansk, Walesa's illegally imported flared jeans and how he envied his moustache. Believe me, General J. was in a mess. When we took him to the disco, and as an introductory punishment asked him to dance alone to 'Saturday Night Fever', he just shrank away, wouldn't enter the spirit of the weekend at all. It was only later when we laid on a pantomime with a Motown theme, with J. playing the part of Berry Gordy that we got some inkling there was life on Planet Jaruzelski. He became attached to the shades the make-up department gave him for the part, that are now the hallmark of his kooky international image. The panto broke the ice, and for a short while it was get down and boogie-woogie time. It turned out J. was big on the Merseysound, 'U Kdod Djz's Jlwak' ('A Hard Day's Night') having just been released in Poland, and he insisted on grabbing the microphone and belting out old Beatles and Gerry and the Pacemakers hits for several hours. It was only when our resident psychotherapist disguised as a 'swinging' DJ managed to wrestle J. through a concealed door and into 'Shampoo', our 360-seater hairdressing salon, that we progressed him on to the next leg of his punishment. It was while presiding Warren Beatty-style over the salon and the bevvy of beauties we had arranged to be there, that we got a little worried about J's motivation towards the whole concept of the weekend, and to tell the truth I'm not altogether sure he recovered the positive attitude he had briefly attained earlier in the day. Certainly results in Poland over the last few years would seem to indicate that General Jaruzelski is one of the few people that the Reward-Punishment Program™ cannot claim as a total success.

Fidel Castro, however, was one of our most successful celebrity guests. He badly needed some R & R (Rest & Relating) away from Soviet tractor quotas and his country's spiralling economy. From the moment his official Cuban Airways Dakota touched down at Albuquerque, we decided he would be treated to an all-American weekend experience. Fidel was mugged twice before he made it out on to the freeway to hitch a ride to the Zipper, and unluckily for him the truck he thumbed down was driven by Julio Jimenez, a large bitter and twisted ex-resident of Castro's island paradise, and long-time Zipper employee. Jimenez had been encouraged to rough him up so much so that the bedraggled figure tossed out of the truck late Friday night in front of the main gates scarcely resembled the bearded *hombre* we had come to know and love. We kept up the pressure remorselessly: a couple of hours as a short order chef in our greasy spoon, serving breakfast to relief workers on the ranch, followed by a stint as a hot-dog salesman at Saturday's impromptu ball game, more than persuaded Fidel his best interests lay in the direction of international co-operation, and relating to people on a one-to-one basis. After that he was into the home straight and there only remained the award ceremony pinning medals on to Bay of Pigs veterans and the giant exploding cigar, before our Third World hero was being tucked up into bed, with a goodnight kiss from Margerita who also had the privilege of serving Fidel breakfast in bed on Sunday morning, before escorting him to the jacuzzi for an extended whirlpool massage. The highlight of Fidel's last day was the opportunity to roundly abuse a deputation of Brezhnev-era Soviet agronomists from Kharkov, before his official send-off at the airport late Sunday night.

But what of the thousands of 'unknown' celebrities that have passed through the Zipper's portals over the years? Let Chuck Chicassa, once a realtor from Florida, speak for them about his experiences. 'The brochure had forewarned me I was in for a challenging time, but boy I didn't realize how challenging! After checking in Friday night, I thought this must be paradise. Unlimited chicks, lines of coke from here to Mars and the finest wines and foods the planet can boast. It was like the last days of Rome.

Little did I realize I was going to be thrown to the lions. In the early hours of Saturday morning the door to my suite is kicked in, and I have my introduction to Crake, this totally evil Marines Sergeant. Before I know it, I'm being ordered round a vicious assault course in the company of guess who?' Here Chicassa breaks into a strange giggle, 'Ronald Reagan! With Sergeant Crake's stopwatch against us we'd made it through the barbed wire and Dobermann kennels with raw meat strapped to us, and were negotiating the Zipper's notorious 'gator swamp, when this crazy old dude and starts reciting his lines from old B-movies! I couldn't believe it. After twenty minutes of this we were out of the swamp and skipping our way through the final hurdle of the minefields. We made it against the clock with seconds to spare. Or thought we had. Crake insisted our delay in the swamp had invoked a penalty clause, and both of us had to perform in a Charles Aznavour-style singing contest. Surprisingly Ronnie had been a big fan of Aznavour's since his days in Hollywood, and he trumped my lukewarm "Sing Little Birdy" with a superb rendition of "She" performed with exotic octogenarian gyrations. Ronnie was into reward time after that, scuttling off for a Big Mac, leaving me as the loser in the contest with one more punishment to undergo: an ice-skating combo with Liberace. It was a nightmare. I thought it would never end. But it did. And you know what? It changed my whole life. I figured anyone who'd partnered Ronald Reagan round an assault course of that severity and had the Liberace experience on ice could handle just about anything life threw at them.

'And believe me life *has* thrown everything at me. A major condo deal I was working on in the Everglades literally sank before my eyes. I was declared bankrupt. My wife and kids left me. I now live in a parking lot in Orlando. But I truly feel that my CRPW™ experience at the Zipper has made me strong and resilient and able to cope.'

So. There you go. And thank you, Chuck, for your unsolicited recommendation. There will always be a place for you at the Zipper, just as soon as you get yourself back on your feet.

The Celebrity Reward-Punishment Program™ is my life, and it becomes part of each and every life that graces our portals.

Sometimes I sit on the porch of our 43-bedroomed Southern Colonial-style mansion, looking out towards the 'gator swamp and the verdant slopes of beautiful Mount Zipper, and I look back at the good times, the hard times, the times I just didn't know if we could come through. And then I think, watching the sun go down behind the Nancy Reagan aerobics center, hey, we made it, didn't we? The Zipper is Success City, USA. We all learnt to relate to each other through Punishment and Reward™ and it feels great!

I first met Mike Machola at a party thrown by Sheri Brillo (see Chapter 8). As he gazed mysteriously into my eyes I felt all of the power of the supernatural open up before me. At the time I was dating a Playboy gatefold girl, but a little uncertain as to the future of our relationship. Mike advised me we were super-compatible, and the fact that our marriage lasted for over a year persuaded me just how brilliant a man he is.

The Astral Guide To Permanent Partnership
by Mike Machola

The search for a permanent partner is no longer the carefree, pleasurable pastime it once was. Today single men and women everywhere are carefully measuring the pros of playing the field against widely publicized, and dangerous, cons. And, unhappily, many are buying the total celibacy ticket, while others check out the action sporting more latex than a grove of Malaysian rubber trees.

But stop! My unique astral projections and databank of individual sign characteristics can guide you to achieving that very special partnership. Just study which sign's characteristics marry best with yours, and you're on your way to happiness the permanent Mike Machola way.

ARIES: March 21st–April 20th
Arians are immature and spiteful individuals who never attain adulthood. As a result their search for a permanent relationship is a difficult – though not impossible – task. Let's look at the options.
Aries/Aries
Yes, you'll enjoy your joint shopping sprees at toyshops, but there are going to be arguments about who plays with the baubles when you get home. A twosome fraught with potential *angst.*

Aries/Taurus

Your juvenile fascination with fun and games is going to be hogtied by this monumentally boring creature from the House of Bull.

Aries/Gemini

The House of Gemini is not only the House of the Twins, it is also the House of Deceit and Theft. This person will exploit you and steal your toys.

Aries/Cancer

Cancerians' moody introspection is going to be a definite minus, but their preoccupation with hobbies and balsa wood models does have some connection with your own kindergarten activities. On balance however, no.

Aries/Leo

You're a show-off, but we're talking a mega-Caesar's Palace style show-off here. Your essentially fragile ego couldn't cope with a Leo.

Aries/Virgo

These people are creepy. They harbour a fastidious regard for cleanliness and health that is downright unnatural. Despite the safe sex, a definite no.

Aries/Libra

The position of Jupiter on the axis looks favourable, *on paper*. But you couldn't handle the dreadful Libran indecisiveness.

Aries/Scorpio

Scorpios are killers, harbouring in their cold hearts dreams of world domination and other twisted, ruthless schemes — in which you would certainly play the role of pawn. Forget it.

Aries/Sagittarius

The clumsiest sign in the firmament. Sagittarians would trample on your Lego, and frighten your hamsters. No.

Aries/Capricorn

No. 1 social climbers. And you're not bright or 'sophisticated' enough to go along for the ride.

Aries/Aquarius

Air & Fire look like a good mixture, particularly as Uranus is in the frame. Aquarians are weak people with an inbuilt fascination for fads — theirs and other people's — which is where there's a percentage in it for you. Given the prospect of endless indulgence by your partner, this pairing is a serious possibility.

Aries/Pisces

Pisceans make Aquarians look like a *corps d'élite*: for these helpless, miserable creatures are unimaginably weedy. The bottom rung of the astrological ladder, and even for you a wholly inappropriate partner.

The Machola Choice – Aquarius.

TAURUS: April 21st–May 21st

Taureans are the most boring and conventional people in the world. No one has ever considered landing a Taurean to be a catch, so you're going to have your work cut out finding a permanent partner. Let's look at it.

Taurus/Aries

A cosmic no-no. Arians are far too impulsive and hedonistic for you.

Taurus/Taurus

Finally you've found someone who knows as much about daytime soaps as you do. And since when did you meet a member of the opposite sex who enjoyed wearing Hush Puppies?

Taurus/Gemini

Within minutes of meeting this person your TV wax lamp and set of kidron-bound *Reader's Digests* will have disappeared. Avoid.

Taurus/Cancer

These dreamy introspective hobbyists won't intrude much on the boring tedium of your daily life. The planetary positions of this alignment look quite attractive.

Taurus/Leo

You're far too dull for a Leo.

Taurus/Virgo

An earth/earth pairing. But this is the only similarity, and in time you would grow to dislike your fastidious Virgoan mate.

Taurus/Libra

The dithering indecision will get to you, but you can control someone like this.

Taurus/Scorpio
You have no real need to share your life with a devious and brutal manipulator.

Taurus/Sagittarius
There's very little upstairs with a Sagittarian, and their clumsy attempts to ingratiate themselves with everybody could not fit in with your lifestyle.

Taurus/Capricorn
If they've thrown in their lot with you, then there's certainly self interest involved. Be very sceptical of this pairing.

Taurus/Aquarius
Absolutely no way. Being driven to the Golf Club or Ballroom Dancing venue in your partner's 2CV with 'Nuclear Power No Thanks' stickers plastered over it is not your idea of fun.

Taurus/Pisces
These people are dreadful. Avoid.

The Machola Choice – Taurus.

GEMINI: May 22nd–June 21st
While the natural tendencies of a Gemini are never anything less than criminal, some of those that belong to this duplicitous sign of the Twins do have the ability to disguise their true natures beneath a smooth-talking patina. Don't believe a word of it.

Gemini/Aries
The naïveté of an Arian is ripe for criminal exploitation, under-lined by the Air/Wind combination. This person could be useful for you.

Gemini/Taurus
Taureans are strangers to anything unconventional and are unlikely to play a part in your grand scheme to pull off the heist of the century.

Gemini/Gemini
A good relationship is based on trust, so no prizes for guessing this one is going to have its problems.

Gemini/Cancer
You will play the dominant role here but despite the advantages of this, you'll be upset by the wildly changing moods of your emotional partner.

Gemini/Leo
Leos have the sort of tawdry glitter that you find attractive. But remember — these people are gross materialists and will soon be spending your ill-gotten gains.

Gemini/Virgo
Suspicious by nature, a Virgo is going to be on to your shady activities very quickly. Not a good security risk.

Gemini/Libra
You can't handle these inconsistent buffoons.

Gemini/Scorpio
An unpleasant Air/Water combination — cross a Scorpio and you could end up part of a motorway.

Gemini/Sagittarius
You can cheat at will on this person. But is that healthy? A poor planetary conjunction here.

Gemini/Capricorn
You're up against someone brighter and much more vicious than you ever will be and, unlike you, sophisticated enough not to wear snakeskin shoes. It won't work.

Gemini/Aquarius
Aquarians want Alternative lifestyle with a capital A. Somehow soyabean yoghurt and free-range goats don't mix well with the Marbella bank-robbing classes you associate with.

Gemini/Pisces
A totally malleable partner, of course, but unfortunately a completely ineffectual one as well.

The Machola Choice — Aries.

CANCER: June 22nd–July 23rd
Cancerians are famous for their wildly changing moods — their deep depressions followed by over-the-top hilarity. This is a deeply insecure and worried sign.

Cancer/Aries
You haven't the consistency of character to handle an Arian's endless self-gratification.

Cancer/Taurus

Are you going to behave when your Taurean partner goes off to whist drives and bingo nights? Unlikely.

Cancer/Gemini

On the face of it a not unreasonable partnership if – and this is a big if – Jupiter aspected Saturn at the nativity. If it didn't, forget it. Did it?

Cancer/Cancer

You can rave and screech at each other or be deeply moody and listen to Leonard Cohen together.

Cancer/Leo

A Water and Fire arrangement. No prizes for guessing which one you are. It won't work.

Cancer/Virgo

Remember it's safe sex with these health-obsessed people, but is it the kind you like? Would you enjoy being forced to wear surgeon's overalls and gloves before making love?

Cancer/Libra

A diurnal Mars/Pluto line up. That plus the fact that your Libran partner is bound to have severe dandruff should put you off.

Cancer/Scorpio

You're just live bait to this shark of the cosmos.

Cancer/Sagittarius

These people are always stepping in dog messes. Do you need it?

Cancer/Capricorn

You're going up in the world with this little raver, and up in snakeskin 'n' tuxedo style too. You need a break. Go for it.

Cancer/Aquarius

Your fragile sense of security is going to be badly dented by a radical Sixties-obsessed freak who still wears Loons and Afghan coats.

Cancer/Pisces

Watching TV is about the most exciting thing you and a Piscean could do together. You have been warned.

The Machola Choice – Capricorn.

LEO: July 24th—August 23rd

Leos are deeply in love with themselves and it's been said that their ideal partner in life is a full-length mirror. However, few are contented with this long term and most want an animate mate. They are appalling show-offs and wear gold spandex clothes.

Leo/Aries
The Sun (Leo) eclipses Mars (Aries).

Leo/Taurus
There's no room for excitement in this stifling suburban conjunction. And excitement in life is what you crave.

Leo/Gemini
Watch out. Geminis are smooth talkers with an eye on tawdry riches.

Leo/Cancer
You have neither the patience nor the inclination to handle this emotional bimbo.

Leo/Leo
You couldn't cope with someone as self-regarding as yourself.

Leo/Virgo
These strange, twisted little people are no proper match for a glamorous, macho big cat like you.

Leo/Libra
Pro: You can take real advantage of the indecision so prevalent in Librans.
Con: Is this the sort of person you want to be seen around with?

Leo/Scorpio
A Scorpio will be singularly unimpressed by your showing off.

Leo/Sagittarius
You've landed up with a total meathead — but luckily this meathead is really sold on your tawdry image. No one ever said Sagittarians were perceptive. And did you know only three Sagittarians in recorded history have been able to count to twenty?

Leo/Capricorn
Possibly because of the influence of Saturn at the nativity, more likely because they're snobs, Capricornians are very socially aware. And certainly aware enough to avoid taking someone

dressed entirely in gold spandex to top-notch society do's.
Forget it.
Leo/Aquarius
Your flagrantly materialist image is going to go down like a cup
of cold sick at the extreme Left Alternative venues favoured by
Aquarians.
Leo/Pisces
These people are chronically inadequate, and virtually invisible.
Not the type of partner you are looking for.

The Machola Choice – Sagittarius.

VIRGO: August 24th–September 23rd
Virgoans are small, bossy, hypercritical, obsessed with personal
hygiene and extremely mean. These characteristics, underlined
by the triune of Saturn, Mars and Jupiter at the ascendant,
ensure that Virgoans are unpopular.
Virgo/Aries
You will continually be spanking your partner for naughtiness.
You enjoy this, and so, secretly, does your Arian mate. But is this
shared activity the basis for a long-term commitment?
Virgo/Taurus
The sheer laziness and boring conformity of your Taurean
partner is going to upset you.
Virgo/Gemini
The fact that a number of your most precious possessions start
disappearing soon after your liaison commences will arouse
your suspicious nature.
Virgo/Cancer
A Mercury-Moon pairing that looks superficially kosher. Beneath
the surface, however, lie deep dissimilarities that are not
favourable.
Virgo/Leo
You will be staggered by a Leo's wild spending sprees, which
will appal your mean nature.
Virgo/Virgo
The planets are perfectly aligned for this match if – and I'm
talking crazy chances here – the Milky Way was correctly
aspected at the solstice.

Virgo/Libra
Librans are very pliable and you will definitely be in the driving seat in this relationship.
Virgo/Scorpio
One bossy word from you and your Scorpio companion is reaching for the jump leads. Not a nice partnership.
Virgo/Sagittarius
You can do better than teaming up with this bit-part player from *Conan the Barbarian*.
Virgo/Capricorn
Your sharp nature has never made you easy socially and you will not therefore be the type of companion a Capricorn looks for.
Virgo/Aquarius
Sexually this is a complete non-starter.
Virgo/Pisces
You desperately need friends, and here is someone in the same position. You have got yourself an utterly slavish admirer here.

The Machola Choice – Pisces.

LIBRA: September 24th–October 23rd
Sexually insecure and in some cases actually hermaphrodite, ingratiatingly smarmy, heavily into dandruff, and unable to make decisions, there are no prizes for guessing that Librans are looking for lucky breaks in life.
Libra/Aries
Even accepting the marginal benefit of Jupiter at the time of birth, this relationship looks fraught with potential problems.
Libra/Taurus
The rigid beliefs and unshakeable conformity of a Taurean give you a badly needed sense of stability.
Libra/Gemini
You may well ingratiate yourself into the arms of a Gemini who will then ingratiate himself or herself into your bank account. Watch out.
Libra/Cancer
You are not secure enough to handle the emotional scenes.

Libra/Leo
You will compete fiercely with a Leo to attract the attention of people you admire. This is unsatisfactory.
Libra/Virgo
Can you handle a fastidious little creep like this?
Libra/Libra
Absolutely nothing constructive can be achieved in this partnership.
Libra/Scorpio
You'll do exactly what your dominant, cruel partner in the black leather mask says. Understand?
Libra/Sagittarius
A Venus-Jupiter duo which has dire forebodings, particularly if Pluto gets in on the act. Can you risk it?
Libra/Capricorn
You'll enjoy going up in society on the back of this social-climbing Goat. But beware: the Goat will ditch you when the going gets tough.
Libra/Aquarius
Experimenting with scary drugs, making love potions from nettle compresses and indulging in the odd bit of urban terrorism are not your scene.
Libra/Pisces
Pisceans have less character than laboratory mice.

The Machola Choice – Taurus.

SCORPIO: October 24th–November 22nd
Scorpios are evil, twisted people who harbour dreams of world domination, and to say that they are spiteful and scheming individuals would be to totally understate their characteristics.
Scorpio/Aries
Your element is Fire and your planet is Paraquat. The Aries element is Fire. Don't think for a moment this promises compatibility.
Scorpio/Taurus
This fusty old carpet slipper is hardly likely to enjoy your predilection for the more bizarre types of sexual activity.

Scorpio/Gemini
Geminis will try and involve you with their criminal schemes. You don't want to end up in jail.

Scorpio/Cancer
Cancerians are weak, exploitable people, but there is a reservoir of sneakiness in the Crab character that should make you cautious of this otherwise favourable partnership.

Scorpio/Leo
Do you really want to settle down with a grotesque show-off?

Scorpio/Virgo
Extremely early in this relationship you will find your strange partner very irritating. Avoid.

Scorpio/Libra
There's no place in the Scorpio scheme of world order for ditherers.

Scorpio/Scorpio
You both understand how ruthless and evil you are. This does not make for a relaxing relationship.

Scorpio/Sagittarius
Do you really wish to spend the rest of your life with someone whose eyebrows meet in the middle?

Scorpio/Capricorn
Your antipathy to people who wear snakeskin shoes and medallions rules this out.

Scorpio/Aquarius
This absurd individual is hardly up your 'strasse'; you'll feel awkward at Amnesty International benefits.

Scorpio/Pisces
This person is just live bait for you and your evil schemes. You want total domination? You're looking at it.

The Machola Choice – Pisces.

SAGITTARIUS: November 23rd–December 21st
Most Sagittarians live alone and sweat a lot. Oafish, sporty and at heart deeply insecure, this is the sign of the Archer – half human and half horse. Many people find it hard telling which is which.

Sagittarius/Aries

You are most at home going for hikes with a backpack weighed down with 350 lb. of rocks. Your prospective Arian partner sees no percentage in this. Very few people do.

Sagittarius/Taurus

Your thrusting outward-bound attitude to life is going to be restricted by this unspeakably boring person.

Sagittarius/Gemini

This person will rip you off very thoroughly. And you aren't bright enough to prevent it. Avoid.

Sagittarius/Cancer

Sagittarians have no aptitude for handling emotional people.

Sagittarius/Leo

Given that you are able to surrender your own ego to the extent that a Leo demands, you're definitely in with a chance with the Big Cat.

Sagittarius/Virgo

The least propitious alignment of all. Your gift for trampling dirt and introducing dust into any environment will drive the cleanliness-obsessed Virgoan up the wall.

Sagittarius/Libra

When it comes to the game of love, these people are just not team players. Besides, what sex is your prospective Libra partner, actually?

Sagittarius/Scorpio

You will be completely outmanoeuvred here as the average Scorpio attempts to perpetrate unspeakable sexual acts on your person.

Sagittarius/Sagittarius

You can blunder around with someone just as clumsy as you. But with the combined intelligence of a subnormal bullfrog you have trouble aplenty ahead.

Sagittarius/Capricorn

In the unlikely event you catch the eye of the Goat, greedy bearded jaws will soon go to work on whatever wealth you may have accumulated.

Sagittarius/Aquarius

The gritty survivalist image so popular with Sagittarians of both sexes — army surplus clothes, Bowie knives, etc — simply does not gell with that of the Aquarian for whom fashion began and ended at Haight Ashbury in '67.

Sagittarius/Pisces
Few people actually hate you, and someone somewhere could learn to love you. So stop and think before doing something really stupid — like getting involved with a Piscean.

The Machola Choice — Leo.

CAPRICORN: December 22nd–January 20th
These cunning inhabitants of the Tenth House of the Goat are deceitful social climbers. They forge business diplomas and wear snakeskin shoes and hairpieces. They will weasel their way into everything and anything, provided there's a percentage in it for them.

Capricorn/Aries
Your ruling planet, Saturn, has never been within the Aries-Mars gravitational pull, and this is reflected in extremely poor prospects for this relationship.

Capricorn/Taurus
Conventional, gullible Taureans make superb targets for your wheedling, deceitful schemes.

Capricorn/Gemini
Both signs are odious and untrustworthy. A partnership where you understand each other only too well.

Capricorn/Cancer
Much of your life is dedicated to social advancement and your prospective Cancer partner will cling to you as you go up the greasy pole. The load's too heavy.

Capricorn/Leo
Plenty of favourable aspects in this Sun/Saturn pairing. The Leo craves flattery and attention and loves to be seen as generous and fashionable. You crave status and money. Work it out for yourself.

Capricorn/Virgo
Life with this uncharitable hygiene-obsessive is going to be very grim.

Capricorn/Libra
Can you handle the ever-changing moods of this inconstant creature?

Capricorn/Scorpio
Earth meets Water. You'll do anything to make a fast buck but where's the action in being hung up by your toenails and beaten with birch twigs? You love yourself. Scorpios hate people. It won't work.

Capricorn/Sagittarius
Failing all else, you could settle for this bumbling simpleton, who all too recently on the evolutionary scale was mutating in swamps.

Capricorn/Capricorn
A double Saturn combination equals double doses of poison. Why ruin your life with someone as unpleasant as yourself?

Capricorn/Aquarius
You love money, designer goods, expensive restaurants, big houses and you don't want to earn them the hard way. Aquarians enjoy loon pants, Polish tractor movies and frisbees. Forget it.

Capricorn/Pisces
Pisceans are so wet they could be poured into a bucket. You've stooped low in life, but not this low.

The Machola Choice – Leo.

AQUARIUS: January 21st–February 19th

Aquarians are always looking for alternative lifestyles, because they are failures in conventional ones. Latter-day hippies, staff of health food shops, UFO fanatics, people who know someone who own a dog which bends spoons, and participants at EST weekends are all Aquarians.

Aquarius/Aries
Having a complex about your own parents, the last thing you want is to be the parent in this relationship, despite the attraction Arians will feel for you.

Aquarius/Taurus

The Taurean lifestyle — one of blissful conformity — is the exact antithesis to yours.

Aquarius/Gemini

A collision of Mercury and Saturn equals two Air signs, thus creating a large vacuum. You are simply not compatible.

Aquarius/Cancer

The native introspection of Cancerians marries well with your hallucinogenically induced introversion.

Aquarius/Leo

Gold lamé, stretch limos and bathfuls of caviar are not your idea of a right-on lifestyle.

Aquarius/Virgo

Virgos won't like the macrobiotic sewage farming you carry on in the kitchen.

Aquarius/Libra

Venus zigzags past Uranus. You're making *all* the decisions here. Can you handle it?

Aquarius/Scorpio

The poisonous Mars/Pluto influence introduces the Scorpio aspect of Paraquat into your life. It's an introduction you don't want. Ever.

Aquarius/Sagittarius

You are cleverer than your gap-toothed partner, and thus able to manipulate this person to participate in your wildly alternative schemes.

Aquarius/Capricorn

You'll be taken to the cleaners.

Aquarius/Aquarius

A match made in heaven. You can sit around knitting macrobiotic socks, listening to old Incredible String Band LPs.

Aquarius/Pisces

Not even you, with your muddled mystical philosophy, want this much peace. This person is virtually invisible.

The Machola Choice — Aquarius.

PISCES: February 20th–March 20th

To describe Pisceans as shallow, spineless and instantly forgett-able would be to overstate their characteristics. These people are virtually invisible.

Pisces/Aries

You simply do not have the resources to cope with the task of looking after this person for 24 hours a day.

Pisces/Taurus

Sexually a non-starter: your water-based Jupiter 'personality' would be unable to withstand the physical ordeal of being loved by the Earth-based Taurean.

Pisces/Gemini

This schizophrenic knave will take you for everything you've got.

Pisces/Cancer

You're even more pathetic than a Cancer, which is saying something. But the alignment of the planets actually looks quite favourable. Be on guard against sneaky deviousness.

Pisces/Leo

Amazingly, this is a favourable pairing. Leos are very self-centred and don't like to be outshone. No chance of that, is there?

Pisces/Virgo

Virgos are very unpopular, and even though this is a far from ideal relationship, they might just make a successful pass at you. This is because they believe that you will fall in with their bossy, shrewish commandments. They're right.

Pisces/Libra

With the combined decision-making ability of a disturbed ant colony, there are no prizes for guessing this pairing scores a total zero.

Pisces/Scorpio

Make a will before accepting a date with a Scorpio. This person wants your body. Probably in little pieces.

Pisces/Sagittarius

These people frighten you with their hairy backs and huge muscles. And as for the men . . .

Pisces/Capricorn

Capricorns need people they can use and — except for some unethical doctors — no one has ever thought of a use for you.

Pisces/Aquarius
The dynamic world of brown rice, lentils, clutch bags and sandals is a little too fast for your liking.

Pisces/Pisces
Finally you've found someone with whom to share your deeply meaningless existence.

The Machola Choice — Pisces.

Once you've met Marti 'Mr Memory' de Bergi, you won't forget him in a hurry. Marti is a sincere man, and a man who not only believes that working on your memory will give you a better life, but who's proved it. Let him prove it for you . . .

How To Develop A Memory
by Marti de Bergi

Congratulations! If you are reading this, you remembered to fill in the form, to sign the money order and to write your correct address. You also remembered your name. You have taken the first steps towards developing a memory — maybe the first steps towards becoming a major success.

Make no mistake about it, having a memory is important. And so many people have no memory at all, and no means of developing one. Nobody has ever succeeded in life without a memory — and the better you remember, *the better you succeed*. Let me start this course with a typical situation.

Walking into a party, you are introduced to half a dozen people: Loraine, Jayne, Dirk, Dick, Dirk, Kirk. Immediately you've forgotten each name — not least because Dirk introduced himself twice! (Or was he a double?) Seconds later and thoroughly confused, your partner joins you. Introductions are difficult not only because you haven't a clue what the people with you are called, but because you've now forgotten your *partner's* name. You could have been together for decades, but your mind is a complete blank. Later in the party someone finds you hiding under the staircase. You don't know:

   a) what your name is;
   b) why this person is talking to you;
   c) why you are crying.

Of course you could be mad, in which case stop reading here. Alternatively, you could well be suffering from a condition which memorologists are now calling the 'social amnesia syndrome'. You're in need of a super-power memory, and unless you can handle the idea of complete social ostracism, you need it fast. From mastering the basics of memorizing your own name, your pet dog's and that of your mother, it is possible to progress to remembering jokes you read in Christmas crackers and your unemployment benefit number. Later as you become more confident, friends and colleagues will appreciate your ability to reel off whole pages from telephone directories and *Exchange & Mart*. But you're lacking in confidence at this stage – as that unfortunate incident at the party demonstrated – and you'll have to go back to basics to *develop a memory*.

To succeed at the memory game, you must actually *want* to remember. For someone like you who has been no stranger to failure and social rejection, this will involve dredging up the many insults, moments of sheer desperation and incidents of grievous bodily harm that have populated your life. Do you have the nerve to do this? If you do, and if you use the notes carefully laid down, in amazingly short time you'll find yourself remembering events you thought you'd managed to blot out forever. The time your parents left you at home because they found you so boring. Turning up at the hoax fancy dress stark naked. The time the Dateline computer rejected your application in preference to its memory bank of 3½ million other people who were – apparently – losing out in life slightly less than you. But let's be positive: you wouldn't be reading this unless you *wanted* to improve your memory, now would you?

The Missing Link System

Read the following paragraph carefully and do *not* make notes.

You are driving your white Chevette along a backstreet. Two men appear and flag you down. One of them is carrying a blowtorch, the other a sledgehammer. You are too terrified to leave your vehicle. The man with the sledgehammer smashes your headlights and demolishes your left wing, as the man with the blowtorch applies this flaming weapon to your rear tyres. While the man with the sledgehammer smashes your roof in, the man with the blowtorch smelts his way into your locked car boot and removes your fire extinguisher. The man with the sledge-hammer then smashes your windscreen, and you and the inside of your car are sprayed with foam. Laughing, they steal your wallet and leave, not before stripping the 'I ♥ Dan Quayle' sticker from your rear window.

Now, without looking at the above paragraph, can you remember whether:

(a) Your headlights were smashed *before* or *after* your left wing was destroyed?
(b) Which of these mischievous gentlemen sprayed you and the inside of your car with foam?

You find it difficult to *remember* the answers to (a) because this type of thing happens to you the whole time and you were *distracted* by reading what you thought was a piece of your personal history!

You are *confused* by the correct answer to (b), which was in fact a trick question as neither of them could resist spraying you with foam: they *both* did it!

Well, award yourself poor marks on that one, but don't despair, there is a way of recalling events if you use THE MISSING LINK SYSTEM.

What you do is identify a single strand connecting through a series of bewildering incidents. Suddenly, you realize that the strand you are looking for is a colour, and the colour is *white*.

Think about it. You were driving a *white* Chevette. There were *white* road markings on the street. Your two assailants were both *white* men, and your tyres were *white*wall. Both you and the inside of your car were covered in *white* foam from the extinguisher. To underline the imagery of colour, as they left they called you '*yellow*'.

Using the Missing Link System turn back to page (70), and see if you can't improve your answers to questions (a) and (b) above.

Having mastered this very basic system, you will now be able to move on to *Key Words*.

The Key Word Memory System of Card Playing

This is one of the oldest systems of memorizing and it may well be the one to work for you.

Many of the greatest poker players in the world employ it — and it's no coincidence that these guys are winners, while people like you couldn't win a game of snap with a blind man.

The trick is to associate each number and each suit with an easily remembered key object. For diamonds, say, a lot of big-time Vegas-style high-rollers find it easier to think of rubies. The connection is obvious. Now all you need is to remember the numbers. But let me stress that there's no point in even trying this if you don't *want* to win. So. Here we go. Many of the Casino world's most brilliant characters use *other numbers* for their key words: one = twelve, two = eleven, and so on. Thus, Five of Diamonds, normally so hard to remember, trips easily off the tongue as Sixteen of Rubies. Easy, isn't it? But if you prefer, and a lot of big-shot gamblers do, you can use objects as *key words*. Thus *Clubs* = Dromedaries, *One* = Trousers, *Two* = Escritoire, *Three* = Bikini-line hair remover, and so on. Work it out for yourself! You're playing chemin-de-fer for big, big stakes at the Playboy Club. The man next to you draws a Four of Spades and an Ace of Hearts. The croupier bends forward and you can see her tits. What's your next card? If you don't have a system, you may never know. Here's *my* simple *key word* chart for Card Sharps!

1	—	Frisbees
2	—	Winkle-Pickers
3	—	Twins
4	—	Bunny
5	—	Smock
6	—	Sock
7	—	Cock
8	—	Bantam
9	—	Frisbees
10	—	Pogo-Stick
Jack	—	Jack
Queen	—	La Rue

King	—	Vidor
Spades	—	Splendid
Clubs	—	Playboy
Hearts	—	Lonely
Diamonds	—	Double
Ace	—	Hearts

Don't be intimidated by playing with the high-rollers. Let's just take it easy and talk our way through the first hand:

Dealer deals you a Seven of Spades, a Four of Clubs, a Ten of Hearts, a Two of Diamonds and an Ace of Hearts. Normally, you'd have lost already and your money would be disappearing into the Casino's strongbox. But now, with the Key Word Memory System, you're on to a winner and it becomes absurdly easy to remember your hand. Let's go over it — you are holding:

A Splendid Cock
A Playboy Bunny
Double Winkle-Pickers
A Lonely Pogo-Stick
An Ace of Hearts

You throw down your Splendid Cock and pick up a Double La Rue. You pick up a Lonely Sock, giving you a pair, and a Double Pogo-Stick. Now you discard the Double Winkle-Pickers, picking up two Frisbees the while. Mistake. You now realize you must throw away the Frisbees, which you do, but too late. Your opponent trumps you with a big pair of winning Playboy Cocks. Unplayable. You have lost:

(a) the game;
(b) a great deal of money;
(c) your membership of the Casino;
(d) all credibility.

But don't despair, at least you've begun to get the gist of the *Key Word Memory System*. Pretty soon you'll wonder how you ever got along without it.

The Road to Success Through the Power Memory

The brain works in mysterious ways. Everyone has experienced weird manifestations of its ability to 'flash back' information at the oddest times: walking past an aromatic baker's shop you remember the breakfasts of your childhood; driving down a leafy lane you remember your first teen-age kiss; stepping into the office and feeling the warm central heating on your legs, you remember you haven't put any trousers on. Make no mistake, the mind's a funny thing. In fact, the pre-eminent Belgian memorologist, Loomis van der Smelter, has worked out that if a computer was constructed with the same capacity as the human brain, it would be terrifically big. Yet it is also said that we actually use only about a millionth of our brain! That's less than the size of a frozen pea!

So. How do we harness this enormous power? The trick is connecting different parts of your head.

Looking at it very simply, your brain is actually divided into two halves — a creative intellectual side and a thrusting practical 'go-getter' side. Only *connect* these two halves — or 'rooms' — and 'success' hormones are released into your body.

You will then find yourself to be:

a) Tremendously attractive to the opposite sex.
b) Very wealthy.
c) Awfully popular.
d) Extremely creative.

It is assumed that you are none of the above at present.

Let's look at a few classic examples.

a) *The Totally Interconnected Brain*
   (This person is awash with success hormones)
   Owns New York City department store, small Caribbean island and most of Devon. Fabulously wealthy. Also bestselling international novelist and Palme d'Or winner at Cannes Film Festival for highly praised obscure subject. Very amusing and attractive to opposite sex. Good looking; self confident.

b) *The Semi-Connected Brain*
(Success hormone quotient not high)
Owns detached house in Zanesville. Works for middle-ranking financial analyst company. Career prospects, now looking iffy. Owns ugly partner and Ford Pinto. Not good at telling jokes. Losing hair and confidence.

c) *The Completely Unconnected Brain*
(Success hormone quotient @ 0%)
Not a homeowner. Works in clerical department of paper-clip supply company. Career prospects zero. Seen eating hamburgers on the street. No manners. Bad skin. Bad hair. Owns three Bon Jovi albums. No car. Used as dartboard by friends' children.

In this memory course, I am never going to lie to you. I have to make it clear at this point in time that *you are never going to make it to category (a)*. Success hormones don't come cheap, either in terms of money or commitment. Category (b) may be your bag. Even that would be a huge achievement for someone like you, so don't downgrade it. For those of you who never want to leave (c) — I advise you to crawl back to the primeval swamp where you belong. Now let's look at some more techniques.

The Date Test
This is a complex examination requiring a high degree of historical and show biz know-how. You can improve your memory, concentration and knowledge of history with this exclusive Date Test. Go for it, your brain cells are on trial!

Part One
Take 2 minutes to absorb the following 15 facts.

1. 1972 Slade get number 1 hit with 'Feel The Noize'.
2. 1966 LBJ endorses US involvement in Vietnam.
3. 1962 Margaret Thatcher sings backing vocal on Helen Shapiro's 'Walking Back To Happiness'.
4. 1711 Ronald Reagan born in Mooskjaw, Miss.

5. 1886   Invention of pocket calculator.
6. 1983   Alice Cooper starts work as golf pro in California.
7. 1411   Black Death decimates Milton Keynes.
8. 1986   Mikhail Gorbachev inaugurates new multi-million-rouble ice-rink in Archangel.
9. 1983   Richard Nixon plays Porgy in Broadway production of *Porgy 'n' Bess*.
10. 1509 Russians launch first dog in Space.
11. 1846 Garibaldi perfects new biscuit recipe.
12. 1936 Solzhenitsyn learns to play the oboe.
13. 1959 Japan beats China 36–0 in first underwater ping-pong international.
14. 1960 Chinese ping-pong players allowed to wear aqua-lungs. Second Japan vs. China international held. Japan vs. China. Japan trounces China 24–1.
15. 1961 Leading Chinese sub-aqua ping-pong players executed in Mao sports purge.

Memory Lesson

Alright? Now close your eyes and without cheating, write down these extraordinary events and facts, using the memory and key word system you have learnt.

1.
2.
3.
4.
5.
6.
7.
8.
9.
10.
11.
12.
13.
14.
15.

Well, aren't you the little smartass! Award yourself ... points out of 15. You have now completed the first part of the Date Test.

Part Two
Some of these facts are true; others are not. Try quoting all of these so called 'facts' on *University Challenge* or *Mastermind* and you'll be in real trouble! Part Two of the Date Test obliges you to *relearn* and *distinguish fact from fiction*, and will require all of your new-found skills.

Read the following partly revised facts carefully and compare with those on pages 75–76:

1. A complete lie – Slade got nowhere with 'Feel The Noize' in 1972.
2. Both Lyndon *and* Lady Bird Johnson endorsed US involvement in Vietnam in 1966.
3. Unaltered fact.
4. Reagan actually born in 1712.
5. Incorrect – pocket calculator actually invented by Leonardo da Vinci in 1560.
6. Unaltered fact.
7. A complete lie – Milton Keynes not built until 1960s.
8. Unaltered fact.
9. Incorrect – Richard Nixon played Bess in Broadway production of *Porgy 'n' Bess*.
10. Unaltered fact.
11. Unaltered fact.
12. Incorrect – Solzhenitsyn learned to play slide guitar in 1936.
13. Unaltered fact.
14. Unaltered fact.
15. Unaltered fact.

Now take a pen and write down the *true* facts and events together with the *correct* date.

1.
2.

3.
4.
5.
6.
7.
8.
9.
10.
11.
12.
13.
14.
15.

Award yourself what I hope will be a splendidly high score and consider yourself one of the 'in' crowd, capable of stunning acquaintances with the ability to memorize fabulously useful facts.

More Memory

So, now we have mastered the basic techniques of memory-improvement, the last thing to learn is how to *use* the memory in business and social situations.

No longer will you clinch a deal and pull out your pen to sign the contract, only to find you have forgotten your name. No longer will you remember to buy flowers on your wedding anniversary, but forget that you are divorced. In short, you will be a new, more dynamic person.

Say you're at a party and you're attracted to a man who's talking football with his friends. Why not sidle over and name the Pittsburgh Steelers team of 1938? And follow it up with a full list of winners and runners-up in the Superbowl since its inception. You're bound to go down a storm with the boys.

Or imagine you've finished work at the office and find you have some time to spare before your train. Why not memorize a page or two of the Yellow Pages (using the infallible systems you've learned) and amaze your colleagues next time they need a dog-do scoop manufacturer or carpet shampoo. Be assured there's always room for someone who can recite a telephone directory in any business organization.

Later on you will be able to recite *The Perfumed Garden* in Arabic at smart dinner parties and then continue to hold your audience over coffee and liqueurs with *The Brothers Karamatsov* word for word. Make no mistake, it paid me to develop a memory, and it can pay you as well.

I first met Sheri Brillo at the White House, in the Sixties. On my right was Lady Bird Johnson, on my left, Sheri. Guess who I talked to all night? Lady Bird was a fantastic conversationalist. But ultimately, it was Sheri who claimed my attention. She has continued claiming my attention at parties across the globe ever since. Sheri is good to her friends. Let her be good to you.

Successful Parties

by Sheri Brillo

'Let's give a party,' someone says. It sounds so simple, doesn't it? But it isn't. Parties are complicated events, and you've got to be smart to handle them. And remember that *you* are going to be judged on just how successful your party is.

There are lots of different kinds of parties, and I've been to them all. There's the dinner party, the birthday party, the surprise party, the kids' party, the one-on-one party, the stag party, even — heaven help us — the funeral party. Which reminds me of a White House party — what a load of stiffs!

Your first task as the 'host or hostess with the mostest', is to decide exactly what kind of party is right for you. Match the type of party to the type of guest. Hell's Angels, for instance, are normally reluctant to wear tuxes, and like to ride motorbikes across dining room tables, so don't go upmarket with them. Equally State Governors and Senators are unlikely to enjoy lounging around on beanbags with hippies discussing the merits of Nepalese Gold.

I didn't get to be the Western world's No. 1 hostess by throwing second-rate parties. My advice to you is to either do it the Sheri Brillo way, or don't do it at all. As Burt Reynolds once said to me, 'There are only two types of party, the absolute stinker or a Sheri Brillo party.' Thank you, Burt. Of course I can't actually invite people like you to my parties, and I can't appear at yours (unless you're prepared to pay my standard $100,000 attendance fee), but I can give you the next best thing: the Sheri Brillo Successful Party Program. Now read on.

The Invitation

The telephone is tacky. If you want to impress in modern party-going society, the very least you have to start with is despatching a Hockney engraving with the party details on the back, or a specially commissioned U2 video with yourself in the lead vocal spot individually inviting a guest list of well over a hundred people that other people are going to want to be seen with. Naturally, everyone wants to be seen around a celebrity. Do you know any? If not, what are you having a party for? Personally, I would simply never throw a party unless I knew for a fact that Tom Jones was in the room.

Thematic Options

(a) The Hobo Thrash

This type of entertainment was popular during the Depression years, which some thought tacky. But now everyone's rich, I can't believe it would give offence.

Insist your friends wear (designer) Skid Row costumes. Get a few tramps off the street to give the evening an authentic flavour (ensure security have them covered). The crowning moment of the evening is when you and your mate appear dressed like royalty. One up to you — but it is your party!

(b) Go Mexicana

Definitely a party with a big theme. All you need is a Tijuana brass band, stacks of Taco-Mexburgers, big floppy hats, and some guys with castanets to serve your guests. We first hit on this quaint 'South of the Border' theme for the opening of the Brillo-Reale Hotel in Acapulco. What a night that was! I never forgave my late husband, Ulysses, for messing around with Dolores Van Stamm. And talking of Ulysses, remember the best way for two guests to get acquainted is eating a taco from opposite ends. It breaks the ice. Remember to have the tacos on hand as introductions are effected.

(c) Men Only
We're talking stag parties here, and I've seen my share of them let me tell you! OK, as a lady I always made my appearance late in the evening. OK, so I appeared naked out of a cake. OK, so my role was normally beneath the table crawling round on my hands and knees (particularly when Ulysses was alive). But I've seen enough down there to tell you what men get up to at stags. Not a lot actually. Men are all bull.

(d) The Chuck Wagon Party
Grab your partner by the hand, and come on down to a Chuck Wagon Party!! Remember everyone wears blue jeans, pointy boots, cowboy hats and, I have to tell you this, in Ulysses's case ranchero-style sequinned tights. Still, no need to go into that now.

This is an evening with the accent on Country and Western. There's a whole lot of whooping going on. Greet your guests with a whoop. A lot of very important people are getting into whooping. Remember the '88 Bush/Quayle campaign?

Serve the food and beverages from a chuck wagon. It's vital your guests eat plenty of beans because later on you've scheduled a surprise farting competition. But whatever you've got planned, make sure your Chuck Wagon party is an *informal* Chuck Wagon party. We've had some really crazy nights round our Wagon-style Bar-B-Q. One night we ran out of coal and had to burn $100 bills for warmth! It was either that or Nancy Reagan's dress!!

(e) Giving a Smorgasbord Party
Those boring old Swedes have got one thing right in their lives – the smorgasbord. This tempting buffet is just crammed with goodies – far too good for those clean-living Nordics to keep all to themselves.

Pile the table high with any foodstuff you can lay your hands on, except unopened canned foods – they're not Scandinavian.

Your guests will be crazy for this sophisticated style of entertaining.

(f) A Brunch Party Can Be So Wonderful
Entertaining Sunday mornings after three hours at the Mormon Tabernacle used to be tough. Not any more. Frozen Iowa bulls' balls and fridge-to-oven Chicken à la Rex have seen to all of that. And didn't anyone tell you about paper plates? Or toss 'n' fry waffles? Come *on* now, you're slacking ... Get brunchin'!!

(g) Really Smart Parties
I'm not talking hoe downs here. I'm talking smart — like a brace of Kennedys and Tony Bennett smart. (You've flown them in at great personal expense, of course, but who's to know?) Naturally the evening's a big personal publicity stunt which, if handled correctly, is going to shell out social dividends for decades. So don't blow it.
  Here are the tips:
  1. Dress up rather than down. You're looking at a ball gown. No, I don't mean a gown you go balling in. I mean an evening gown.
  2. Tasteful finger foods are vital during that first — tricky — half-hour. Ulysses favoured trays of erect bananas, but perhaps only someone with his unique personal charisma could carry that one off at a sophisticated party.
  3. When Tony Bennett gets the urge to sing, my tip would be to humour him. But when Teddy Kennedy limbers up for a major choral work, a polite hostess will stage a diversion.

(h) Throwing a Kids' Party
Make no mistake about it, a kids' party says a lot about the parents. Don't even think about doing it on the cheap.
  When Ulysses Jnr was five we hired Disneyland — remember, Disneyworld wasn't built then — and flew in a planeload of his little friends, hired Sinatra for the party sounds, and tossed in world-famous mime artist Marcel Marceau for entertainment. We retained Sardi's for the catering, and they retained world-famous chef Paul Bocuse to make the Jell-O.

Now, I know not everyone can afford this — but who needs Frank these days? That's saving you $1,500,000 for starters. But whatever economies you decide on, when it comes to party bags, don't shortchange the kids. We've got to be talking Cartier.

Party Magic with Canned Foods

I'm *serious*. Not all party food comes straight from the hoof or God's little green acres. Canned foods are not only delicious *and* healthy — they can be invaluable timesavers in an emergency.

One time when I was a teenager at Vassar I was so rushed off my feet I had no time to prepare for the party. So I daringly placed cans of soup and openers opposite each seated guest. And you know what? They loved this challenge to their social etiquette and the evening went wonderfully . . . Proving you *can* make it with canned party magic!

Handling Rudeness at Your Party

Politeness is a virtue. I say this because I get a lot of envy from people arriving in my house, and I don't respect that. If a jealous guest gets rude with me, why that makes me mad enough to eat a skunk. I stamp on it hard. Very hard. The offender is escorted back to the limo park by security.

Sex at Parties

Everybody likes to party, party. And there are some who like to swing at parties as well. OK. Except not at mine. I know you'll have read things about Ulysses, particularly the time with that bitch Suzie Schlock, but I can assure you I never allowed him to go the whole way at any party of mine.

It was during the wake we held for Ulysses — I flew in a few hundred guests to Brillo Theme Park City in New Jersey — that I realized how very important giving parties had become to me, and how I had become the most successful party-giver in all recorded history. (OK, I'll admit Caligula and Nero knew a thing or two when it came to throwing fabulous events, but these days, you can't hire party gladiators or untamed lions and slaves without great difficulty.) That's when I knew I had to share my expertise with you. I know you'll use what I've told you to good effect. Have a great party.

Go anywhere in the world where books are sold and of all the authors on display, the name of Eugene Flaubert III will be the most prominent. Eugene Flaubert has dwarfed the so-called giants of 20th century literature, and indeed reduces Shakespeare to the role of admiring acolyte, in terms of copies sold per annum. Now he shares with you the keys to his amazing writing craft.

Be a Successful Writer

by Eugene Flaubert III, author of *The Girl From Waco*

Do you want to be published? Do you read books and think you could write just as well? Do you yearn to be Jackie Collins or J. T. Edson? Do you want a job which could earn you millions of $s without leaving the comfort of your own home? Unbelievable as it might seem many top writers, like myself, get out of bed at 11.30, type for ½ an hour and plunge into the jacuzzi, the day's work done!

I've now written over 600 episodes of the hit TV series the *Kiwani Kamikazes* and a string of novels, including the multi-million-copy seller *The Girl From Waco*. And it's made me a wealthy man. Very wealthy. Writing can make you wealthy too. And there are dozens of different ways you can turn some spare time, a pad of writing paper and a ballpoint into solid gold.

Let's look at the various types of writing in question.

Writing for the Small Screen

Ten years ago I was invited to script a class police procedural, *Precinct Zero*, for Channel KBUM. The viewing figures for the trailers and pilot were sensational, but it never made it to a regular slot because KBUM couldn't get the advertising revenue. Shame. To this day I still get fan mail for that one pilot. I was writing out of my skin. The dialogue for *Precinct Zero* was gritty and totally authentic. I loved it. Let's look at a slice.

* * *

Officers Weiskopf and Krisp are cruising downtown Chicago when they spot small-time hustler Tony 'The Rat' Rizlo acting suspiciously. Giving chase they corner him in an alley.

Weiskopf: 'Spread 'em, sleezeball.'
(Rizlo bends reluctantly over the bonnet)
Krisp (toying with his nightstick): 'Wider.'
Rizlo: 'Wider?'
Weiskopf: 'You heard him, ginzo.'
Rizlo (protestingly): 'You think I'm some kind of acrobat?'
(Krisp frisks him)
Krisp: 'What do we have here?'
(Removes cellophane packet)
Weiskopf: 'PCP — Angel Dust. They're gonna lock you up and throw away the key unless you talk.'
Rizlo (in a high falsetto): 'OK man. OK. But I need protection. (Slowly) There are some very heavy dudes in on this.'
Krisp: 'Like who, scumbag?'
Rizlo (quietly): 'Like Marvyn Scoggins. Like Joe Baumgarten.'
Krisp: 'The famous Senator?'
Rizlo: 'No, the ballet dancer . . .'
(Krisp smashes Rizlo's head against the hood)
Krisp: 'One more smart remark, Rizlo, and you'll be eating more than an Oldsmobile police cruiser.'
Weiskopf: 'Yeah, Rizlo. What's the story on Baumgarten?'
Rizlo: 'He's got a giant processing plant in Fort Worth. 2000 barrels a month. I'm telling you, it's the truth.'
Krisp: 'It better be, or I'll have your ass. Now get in the car.'
Rizlo: 'I know my rights. You can't do this.'
Krisp (weighing the packet in his hand): 'As of this moment, you don't have any rights.'

It was no surprise the audience loved that pilot. When you're writing stuff like this authenticity is the keynote. *Precinct Zero* wasn't a romantic place. It's a tough world out there. At times a savage one. To beef up on detail, I spent two months courtesy of the Chicago Police Dept, riding rooky with a couple of cops. Weiskopf and Krisp are modelled on them.

I couldn't have written *Precinct Zero* without that experience. This type of writing demands it. Otherwise it'll come over fake. Want to write police procedurals? You've got to:

1. Make the dialogue fast and punchy.
2. Gain experience of what it's really like out there.
3. Ensure the criminals conform to traditional stereotypes.
4. Drop in a few wisecracks, but don't overdo it.

Follow those guidelines and you can't miss. Go away and do it, and tell me I'm wrong.

Writing Historicals

I'm not a proud man. I'll do anything for cash. For instance I've been writing historical romances under the *nom de plume* of Shirlee Bustee for well over thirty years. I'm a big Regency fan myself and twenty of my twenty-five historicals have been set in that glorious period of English history.

Let's look at my personal favourite, *The Powder Blue Perriwig*, and its outrageously good beginning. We'll discuss the ingenious trick I've employed later.

The Powder Blue Perriwig

Chapter One. 'The Cockaded Parrot.'

'Abominable, my lord, abominable,' exclaimed Rodney de la Cute, adjusting his beauty spot by a fraction of an inch, and staring with a shocked expression at the corpulent features of Lord Carteret, who sat slumped in front of him. 'Abominable,' he repeated.

'Yes, indeed,' rejoined Carteret, 'the packet left for France yesterday and my spies in Dover assure me your brother was aboard.'

De la Cute walked over to the cathedral glass window and looked down over the teeming streets of Westminster below. His brother, Montacute, had always been impetuous — an irrational creature given to wild impulses, but *this*! This outrage would sully the name of the de la Cute family for generations.

'How *could* he?' shouted Rodney despairingly, stamping one exquisitely shod foot on the parquet floor, turning to face Carteret, who surveyed him with a sceptical — perhaps even jaundiced — eye. 'How could he?' he cried, tears smearing his Penhaligon's face powder, reducing his almost feminine features to a dough-like consistency. 'How could he?' he whispered, crawling on his knees towards Carteret's gouty legs.

'Come, come,' said Carteret, pulling an exquisitely wrought snuff-box from his heavily brocaded coat pocket. 'What's done is done, and cannot be undone. The packet left for France yesterday and my spies in Dover assure me your brother was aboard.' His businesslike tone, however, was lost on the writhing figure at his feet.

'How could he?' was all that Rodney de la Cute could mouth.

Well, well, thought Carteret. So things have come to this pretty pass. The packet gone, de la Cute aboard. Well, well. Raising himself from his slumped posture, he stepped dismissively over the outstretched figure of the grovelling young man, and took up his station at the window. On the finely inlaid walnut occasional table rested a pair of lorgnettes, a present from the Countess of Dagenham on the occasion of the great victory at Cortina. He took them now, and scanned the crowds below. It was as if he was looking for something, almost without being conscious of looking. Suddenly he stiffened, his eye following a particular young man – a longshoreman or lighterman perhaps, shabbily dressed but tall and . . . somehow haughty, his fine features, for all the grime that caked them, almost like those of a woman. If Carteret hadn't known better, he might have sworn he was looking at none other than Montacute de la Cute. But he did know better. His own spies had told him that the packet had sailed for France, and Montacute with it.

Unless . . .

There's a clever, clever device that I've used in that introduction to 'hook' the reader. Can you guess what it is? No? got it. It's called 'literary repetition', a trick that's been handed down the aeons from Jane Austen to Georgette Heyer. It's a known fact with this type of work, that your characters can't be understood unless they repeat themselves. Endlessly. It works, believe me. By Chapter Ten – you don't get the whole book here, go out and buy it – Rodney has uttered the word 'abominable' 4020 times, and repeated the phrase 'How could he?' 1825 times. Carteret, until his untimely death in Chapter Fifteen, strangled in his sedan chair by a lexicographer, has said 'Come, come' no less than 6051 times. It makes for engaging reading, and has been the hallmark of my historical writing for thirty long years. Pick up your pen and repeat after me, 'I can do it. I can do it.' You *can* do it. Go for it.

Writing Science Fiction

It's the mark of a truly great writer – and by great I mean truly dedicated – that he or she can turn his or her pen, typewriter or word processor to any area of the writing art. Take me, for example. I've encountered just about every kind of writing at one time or another during my thirty-year career. And one of the whackiest areas of this great business we call literature is Science Fiction. But hey, you won't catch me saying, 'Sci-Fi? I just don't understand that stuff — leave it to the experts.' No, sir. Me, I'm always positive. If people want to read it, so be it. I can deliver a Sci-Fi m/s on any goddam subject I like. Anytime. Anywhere. *On* time.

So. How do we make Sci-Fi a part of your repertoire? Science Fiction is the literature of the future. Thus, it's not like real life, and you have to make it — literally — out of this world. Maybe we should look at a little novel I wrote some years ago, which has been acknowledged by many of the Science Fiction greats as a major influence on their lives and on their work.

Return to the Planet of Death opens with ace space fighter Cute de la Rod summoned before Space Lord Car-ter-et in the Martian Spacedrome to answer for the disappearance of a packet of valuable Uranian ray dust.

(Note: Cute is not just an ordinary fighter pilot, but a *space* fighter pilot. It's not just an airport but a *Spacedrome*. And finally, weirdly, brilliantly, we signal the kind of far-out novel we're writing here by placing the action not in London, New York or Rome, but *Mars*!)

'An abominable theft, Space Lord, abominable,' said ace space fighter pilot Cute de la Rod, as he adjusted his Martian jockey shorts for comfort and gazed at the Astroturf at his feet. 'It's absolutely abominable.'

Xenon Car-ter-et, absolute Master and Space Lord of the Universe, relaxed into his Castle-Main XXXX Command sofa and gazed at the guilty young man in front of him. Cute de la Rod would have to go. Mars was a small place. Too small for criminals of indeterminate sex.

'Somewhere out there, de la Rod, is a place you call home,' said Car-ter-et gazing through the giant Viewdrome window at Space in all of its infinite and resplendent glory. 'But it's not here. It's not here,' he repeated drily. 'I want you to leave this planet. You'll be vapourized back to earth within two quargs.'

'How could he?' thought Cute, as he watched Car-ter-et's blotchy hand move inexorably towards the Mimotron quarg vapouriser.

'Stop,' he screamed. 'It wasn't me who stole the packet. It was Zeenix. Zeenix perpetrated this abominable crime. I swear it.'

'Zeenix? Zeenix?' exclaimed Car-ter-et, arresting his hand. 'Well, well. Well, well, well, well, *well*! Zeenix. *Zeenix* of all people. It was Zeenix after all!' His trusty servant Zeenix, who'd been with him all of thirteen and a half centuries. Car-ter-et thought quickly: de la Rod knew too much; Zeenix must have told him everything. 'Sorry, Cute, I don't believe you,' he responded brutally, driving the handle of the vapourizer down, despatching de la Rod into the void.

Fabulous, fabulous stuff, eh? SF is *so* original. I love it. Because it's *unreal* you can experiment with *way-out* inventions like quarg vapourizers! People your stories with characters who have wacky names like Car-ter-et. That's how they do it out there in Space!

Situation Comedy

First, what is situation comedy? Well, it's a drama series of ½-hour shows probably about a family with a Mom, a Dad and a couple of whacky kids who have some great friends who live next door. Every week one or other of them gets into a difficult situation — like Dad forgetting to bring the boss's trousers back from the dry cleaners, and having to get out of it in a funny way, like by lending the boss *his own* trousers and having to walk back from the office in boxer shorts, with Mom and the kids all laughing.

However, not every situation comedy has exactly the same characters. Sometimes you have two guys who room together and date two sisters, or two girls who room together and one of them always dates the great guys and one of them always dates the zeros.

Basically, though, that's advanced comedy and often doesn't work for the networks. To be sure of being screened beginners should start with Mom, Dad and the two kids. If you want to get original, why not throw in a dog? I've been writing sitcoms for the networks for nearly thirty years, and I prefer the basic family set-up, even though I've experimented with other more complex situations.

So, if you want to get into television comedy my advice is

don't rush it. I know it seems like a daunting prospect to be funny for ½ an hour. But maybe, at first, you should aim for the commercial break. You've got the characters already, so just ease them into a funny situation. Say Dad has got two tickets to the ball game and he's going to take his son, but the little girl throws his trousers into the wash with the tickets in the pocket. Hey, that's funny! But only if they get to go to the ball game in the end. If you think maybe the father should have thrown the little girl into the washing machine and then cut up his wife with a razor, because she brought the kid up to be so dumb, then that isn't funny. It's a tragedy, and maybe you should be writing serious drama.

Serious drama

I've been writing serious drama for the networks for well over thirty years. Indeed my first show, *The Smiths of Smoky Mountain County*, is still to be seen syndicated on AFN cable stations as far away as Okinawa and Frankfurt. And my advice to anyone wanting to write serious drama for TV is never forget the basic principles that make drama different from comedy. Let's take some examples. Two couples have babies, and the hospital gets the kids mixed up. *In a comedy*, the cleaning lady would come in to do the room, pick up the babies again and put them back in the right cots by mistake. *In drama*, the kids would grow up to become Presidents of huge oil companies and each would hate their father, until they discovered the horrible truth from the cleaning lady, who would be blackmailing their mothers and sleeping with the paediatrician responsible for the mix-up in the first place. Now that's serious entertainment.

When you've cut your teeth writing a few series for TV, there's no doubt you'll want to move on to the Big Screen. And that means tinsel town. The Big H. Hollywood.

The Movies

Take One. There you are in Southern California. You've rented a high-rent apartment in a low-rent building. Mistake. Lesson one. Never try to live in a room you have to rent by the hour.
Take Two. Poolside at your new building. Less rent, and who

cares that the 'pool', is really only a mini-sized pool table. You've got a pool, right? This is an image-conscious town. Let's keep it that way. OK? Now you've got the scenery to set yourself up, begin your writing career in Hollywood.

There are two kinds of screenwriting. Either you take a book that someone else has written, or even that you've written yourself, and turn it into a screenplay by taking out all the words that aren't dialogue and subtly changing the story, or you can develop a completely original concept. Note this important word 'concept'. You don't just sit down and write a screenplay in Movieland. You develop a concept. From the writing point of view a concept doesn't have to be too long. Say, two lines. I've been a big mover and shaker on the Strip for what, thirty years or more, and I can tell you, if a big studio boss can't read your concept in the time it takes to drop his pants and step over to the casting couch for some important pre-production concept development of his own, then your concept isn't worth the paper it's written on.

So, get yourself a concept: something like – 'Ace detective Tony Mallone stumbles on an ingenious Russian plot to wipe out the United States, by infiltrating thousands of *spetznatz* special forces troops disguised as competitors in the World Water Skiing Championships in Malibu.'

This concept has several great advantages for the men you need to impress in order to get your project into development. Let's look at them:
1. Cheap locations – just drive out to the beach.
2. Great action shots with the water skiing.
3. No expensive sets to build – the ocean comes free.
4. Your super-jock hero gets to spend a lot of time with his shirt off, and there are going to be some fabulous girls around – in bikinis, you bet.

So, having sold the idea, you're in development and you need to go for the full screenplay. How do you write one? Remember, it's not the same as a novel. You're writing for the camera now. For the cameras and actors. And believe me, they're funny people. Actors, that is, not cameras. Hollywood is wacky, but not that wacky yet.

So, why don't we look at the opening page of *Red Beach, Blue Bikini*, the script in question?

Santa Monica. A dazzling afternoon (*movie buffs among you may remember that in the actual production starring Lee Grossman, the opening shot was of a rain storm, but, like they say in Hollywood, that wasn't in the script!*) Tony Mallone sits at the desk of his two-bit detective agency, a battered typewriter and a fifth of rye in front of him. Behind him (*important to set the scene here*):
1. A big picture of Tony on waterskis.
2. A certificate saying 'Tony Mallone — World Water Ski Champion'.
3. A framed newspaper headline which reads 'Tony Mallone's Leg Shot Off in Gangland Shoot Out — Will Never Ski Again'.

The door opens and a really beautiful girl walks in. (*Again fans of the silver screen who actually saw the movie — and there are literally hundreds of you out there — will remember that unfortunately it was Debbi-Anne Debrett who came through the door. Level with the fact your shooting script is never going to be perfectly translated on to the screen and you have to learn to live with a degree of disappointment. In this case a big one. The script said, 'a really beautiful girl', but* the budget *said Debbi-Anne Debrett.*) Malone makes no move to take his feet off the desk. Why should he for this dog? Debrett: (*this is how you write the dialogue*) 'Is that a gun in your pocket or are you Tony Mallone, the monopede ski bum with the twelve-inch wanger?'

Mallone: 'What's it to you, babe? I *used* to be Tony Mallone.'

Debrett (sitting down and pulling out a cigarette). 'Easy, big boy. Everybody knows about the accident. That was one helluva break. But maybe what I've got to say will give you a chance to get your own back on Rocky Caruso.'

Mallone (bitterly): 'Get my own back? My own what? Is Rocky Caruso going to give me back my Water-Ski Championship? Give me back my pride? My leg?'

Debrett: 'Hey, lighten up. I already said I was sorry about your leg. I'm Rocky's girl now. Only I don't want to be. I don't want to go along with his depraved wishes. But I have to. He's holding my sister Arlene hostage. He says he'll kill her if I don't do everything he says.'

(Camera cuts to Mallone who looks interested for the first time in the film). (*And believe me, movie fans, Lee Grossman was interested in this part as he hadn't read this far into the script, as the rest of the film was to prove. I still defend the decision to use Grossman, though. As I said at the time, how many one-legged actors are there who can water-ski, anyway? Grossman was our best shot for the money available. I only wish he could have lived to see the movie.*)

Mallone: 'You don't know where he's hiding her, right?'

(*This is what Grossman actually says in the film, although since this is something of a confidential session, I don't mind telling you that in the first take he said, 'What is it exactly that he makes you do?'*)

Get the picture? I'm sure you do — brilliant writing like that always hooks people. *Red Beach, Blue Bikini* ... I still dream about that movie. It's a masterpiece. I've given you a taste of what it's like out there in the hot-house atmosphere of Hollywood scriptwriting. There's only one thing left to do. Go for it.

Incidental Writing

This is what I call 'pay that bill' writing. The sort of writing you do between novels and screenplays. Early on in my career I tied up a deal with the Wac-O Greeting Card Company — Thanksgiving cards, Greeting cards, Bereavement cards, Sorry-I-Forgot-Your Birthday cards, Graduation cards — you name it, I've done it.

With this type of writing — and it may not be glamorous but it sure brings in the bucks — you've got to recognize that the people buying these cards haven't got the brains to write a message themselves. So you've got to express what they can't. And always remember that the message is better if it rhymes. Let's look at a few examples:

The Birthday Card
... years ago today
Was your birthday.
That day
Was a fun day
For your Mom and Pop.
Let's hope today
Is a fun day
For you
Love
....
OK? Or how about this?
Granny, you're a lot of fun

Even when you're eighty-one
And we all love you, everyone.
You're the apple of our eye
We'll be even happier when you die
Love
. . . .

Graduation Cards
Hey ho, hey ho, it's off to work you go!
You're through with college
And childhood things
Hey ho, hey ho, hey ho, hey ho!
Love
. . . .
Or how about this?
Phi Beta Capa!
We love ya!
Love
. . . .

Thanksgiving Cards
Thanksgiving Day is here again
The turkey it is baking
To look at the family now
You'd be reminded of
A Norman Rockwell painting
Love
. . . .
Or responding to a Thanksgiving Present
My present's just fine and dandy
It'll sure come in handy.
These simple words express
My gratitude
No more no less
Love
. . . .

I think by now you'll have got the picture. Go for it.

Thrillers

What is a thriller?

A thriller is an exciting story with a beginning, a middle and an end. There are many types of thriller. Let's look at it.

The beginning This is critical. Blow your opening and you've had it. Grab the reader's attention straight away. Let's examine the opening to my famous thriller, *The Well-Notched Beretta*.

Secret agent Rockne Strange gasped as Bresinski rotated the handle of the vice, squeezing his balls into closer, uncomfortable proximity. 'You bastard,' Strange whistled through his remaining teeth, 'Wimperis never made it because you poisoned his cake mix. Daktari drowned because you punctured his armbands. Schittelkopf wasted two weeks in Torremolinos while you were in Sarajevo and I was in Bucharest, while Manciewitz ...' 'Manciewitz was me, you fool,' screamed Bresinski triumphantly, rotating the handle rapidly like some demented organ grinder at a Balkan country fair.

That's a fabulous beginning to a fabulous read. What does it tell you? *A lot*. Let's look at it.

1. Strange is a secret agent.
2. His nuts are held in a vice.
3. Bresinski, his opponent, is turning the handle of the vice probably to extract information from Strange, just possibly for the hell of it.
4. Bresinski is a bastard.
5. Strange has lost several teeth.
6. Strange can whistle.
7. Bresinski has murdered Wimperis and Daktari.
8. Wimperis was keen on cooking.
9. Daktari couldn't swim without armbands.
10. Wimperis and Daktari were, by implication, confederates of Strange.
11. Schittelkopf spent two unprofitable weeks in Torremolinos.
12. Strange visited Bucharest during the same period.
13. Strange thought Bresinski was in Sarajevo.
14. Strange was possibly fatally wrong on that because Bresinski reveals he was 'Manciewitz'.

15. Bresinski/'Manciewitz' gets completely carried away on the vice once this information is vouchsafed.
16. Strange is unlikely to be fathering any children in the future.

That opening paragraph is choc-a-bloc with facts. The scene is dramatic and authentic. Several characters are neatly introduced into the plot. It's cosmopolitan and violent — just the way I like it. Let's move the story on.

Bresinski, apart from being a sadistic fruitcake, is also stupid. Very stupid. He rotates the vice the wrong way, thus releasing Strange, who in turn releases him from his mortal coil with a single shot between the eyes from his Beretta.

The action moves to Moscow in Soviet Russia, where Strange eliminates Bresinski's master, the notorious Colonel Vitbe, and half the Politburo, almost precipitating WWIII. It's always vital to set your erotic scenes in the middle of the book, and so, for purely gratuitous reasons, Strange finds himself vacationing in Rio where he meets pouting South American lovely, Dolores del Carmenrola.

The middle

Rockne Strange swept back his hair, throwing into relief his proud features, and leant casually against the bar of 'El Gringo Ringo', the vile lean-to cantina which counted as unsophisticated Rio's most sophisticated joint. Rockne Strange was naked, save for a skimpy pair of bathing trunks and his covering of black springy hair that some would call human, others simian. Rockne Strange was bored. Bored of margeritas. Tortillas. The Americas.

Suddenly a hand explored the twisted undergrowths of his back. 'I want you,' breathed a sultry voice, and, turning, Strange looked into the eyes of Dolores del Carmenrola — the finest-looking woman south of the Rio Grande. 'My pleasure,' he quipped, whistling up another margerita from Pepe, the swarthy squinting barman whose speed of service added another dimension to the word 'mañana'.

Later, as they stumbled into the darkness of his hotel bedroom, Strange heard the unmistakable sound of a woman's breasts being released from their twin harnesses. 'God, you're beautiful,' he muttered as he busied himself exploring the boundless contours of her body, with the broad lascivious gestures of a hungry army on the move — here bivouacking briefly in the glorious slopes of her belly, there investing all his might in the spoiling of her defences. Dolores, too, was anxious to colonize the unknown territory of Strange's body, which she now enjoined with hers in a glorious pounding surge of ecstasy, only pausing briefly to wonder why his testicles resembled flattened *cojoñes*.

The sheer eroticism of that passage still takes my breath away. Notice how I milk the exotic location for all it's worth: the cantina, the margeritas, Pepe — the typical South American male stereotype — and heighten and contrast this effect with Strange's laconic attitude to his surroundings. Strange is, in effect, saying, 'So what? Who gives one?'

But his mood changes from the moment he feels Dolores's hand exploring his back, and hears her unequivocal declaration, 'I want you.' A physical element has been introduced subtly into the story, and the reader will now expect to be taken a stage further. The reader is not disappointed. The couple repair to Strange's hotel bedroom, and they're not intent on a game of Scrabble. Far from it. As they stumble into the room, Strange hears 'the unmistakable sound of a woman's breasts being released from their twin harnesses', so it's clear. Dolores isn't hanging around. Neither is Strange, for within a brief, though unspecified length of time, he is 'exploring the boundless contours of her body' like a 'hungry army on the move'. The action is raw; the passion intense and all too obviously mutual, as Dolores is 'anxious to colonize the unknown territory of Strange's body'. Granted she's perplexed by the shape of Strange's nuts, which resemble 'flattened *cojoñes*', but not perplexed enough to call a halt to proceedings for a detailed inspection.

Perhaps she found them exciting. Perhaps not. We shall never know, for the lovers are then interrupted in their erotic reverie by a hail of gunfire from six heavily armed *pistoleros*. Dolores goes the way of all flesh, cut down in the very act of procreation. Strange is captured by El Sordo and escorted under guard to the sinister Villa Peculiaritas.

Let's move on, inexorably, to the conclusion of *The Well-Notched Beretta*. Escaping the Villa Peculiaritās dressed as a nun, Strange is forced to spend the next three months in deep cover disguised as a Sister of Mercy at a convent high in the Andes. This is a time of reflection and introspection as he ponders the attractions of the contemplative life. Vowing to return one day, after his mission is finished, Rockne Strange departs Latin America via a banana boat to Ocho Rios, Jamaica, thence by Eastern Airlines to Langley for an emotional reunion with austere, haughty CIA boss Samson Buzz Jnr.

Telling him to chuck his habit and don the standard issue CIA Brooks Brothers suit, Buzz lays it on the line for his star agent. The Western world is running out of oil. And America is running out fastest. Strange is to penetrate the highest echelons of the powerful Saudi oil cartel, kidnap King Fauzi and blow his head off unless the Gulf States sign away their entire oil reserves to the US Government in perpetuity.

The end

Gulf Air Flight No. 748 from New York circled Bahrain Airport before manoeuvring into landing position, its huge silver belly glinting in the stark beauty of the harsh desert sun. Secret agent Rockne Strange relaxed into the generous contours of his Al-Huk Class seat, nursing the giant orange juice that had been his constant companion on this dry, dry flight since it had left the wet, wet tarmac of Kennedy ten hours before.

Gazing laconically out the window Strange wondered what it was that turned people on to deserts. To him Arabia was one big beach, without the sea, girls, bikinis and open-top beach buggies he'd known in his Californian youth.

Clearing customs at Farouk-al-Fauzi Royal Airport was a formality, involving only the traditional confiscation of *Eat It Raw*, *Lady Be Nice* and *The Bum Bishop*, Strange's travelling collection of soft porn. Later, as he checked into the air-conditioned luxury of the Dervish Interconti-nental, he reflected on the number of pornographic books he'd had confiscated in his long career. Twenty, thirty thousand? He'd lost count. What the hell did it matter anyway?

The door to Suite No. 1 opened and Strange surveyed the room. It was good to be back. Dismissing the bell-boy with a derisory tip, pausing only to bin the invitation for a complimentary mint tea in the 1001 Nights Lounge, he silently searched the room for bugs. It was clean. He stripped off and relaxed in the whirlpool bath for half an hour, feeling the jet lag ease away. And he needed to be relaxed. Tonight was to be his only chance to meet King Fauzi, at an exclusive reception thrown by oil minister, Sheik Hakri.

Later, at the reception, Rockne Strange surveyed the eddying currents of Saudi social intercourse from his vantage point on the balcony. He sipped at his eighteenth orange juice. Eighteen juices! And he still hadn't met Fauzi. God, what was wrong with this country? 'Mr Strange?' came a silky voice from behind him. Turning, Strange found himself face to face with the man himself — a vast behemoth, resembling nothing more nor less than a tub of spicy Arabian lard. 'Your Highness,' Strange replied, always greeting royalty strictly according to protocol, 'what a magnificent reception. Le tout Bahrain est ici,' he added slipping into French with the ease of a chameleon. 'Me, no what understand you,' muttered Fauzi, a mystified expression clouding his fatty features. 'Maybe you comprenez this,' said Strange brutally, pressing his Beretta against the small of his back. 'Just do as I say, and you'll come to no harm.' So saying Strange propelled Fauzi towards the French windows. 'Smile, you bastard,' whispered Strange as they weaved their way through the crème de la crème of Saudi society, 'smile!' The monarch obliged with a shit-eating grin, as if to say, 'Hell, I can't imagine anything nicer than a walk outside with Rockne Strange without bodyguards.'

On reaching the VIP car park, Strange forced the gorged potentate into his hired Mini-Moke, and covering him with his Beretta, drove off into the desert. Destination? A rendezvous with the Agency beside the Kingdom's only desert phone booth, some twenty miles from the city. This was no time for social pleasantries; conversation was impossible anyway over the sturdy whine of the one-cylinder British Leyland engine.

Strange kept his foot flat on the floor as the powerful machine leapt and bucked its way over the rough desert road. The giant US Navy Sikorsky helicopter was due to rendezvous minutes away, and he had to meet it. Samson Buzz wasn't a man to hang about. At last the phone booth hove into view. Dialling Sheik Hakri's number, Strange waited impatiently for the oil minister to be summoned. 'Tell him,' bellowed Strange as Hakri came on the line, 'tell him about the deal.' Fauzi spoke excitedly into the phone, as Strange heard the unmistakable sounds of descending rotor blades chopping the balmy stillness of the night air above.

'Hakri! Give the Americans our oil,' quavered the terrified monarch. 'Sign it all away. All. A paper has been provided. Sign it now or my head will be off blown.' Strange's source at Hakri's residence confirmed by radio that the deal had been done. The oil was theirs!

The Sikorsky landed in a blizzard of sand. Figures gesticulated at him from the cockpit. Without the oil Fauzi was a dead man anyway. It was better to be cruel than to be kind, thought Strange, pitilessly tossing a grenade into the booth, where the obscenely fat figure struggled to extricate itself. Thirty feet up in the air, Fauzi and phone booth exploded in a dazzling array of colours. 'A drink?' asked Samson Buzz Jnr. 'Don't make it an orange juice,' said Strange with a roar of laughter.

Well, well, well. Breathless? You bet. What a finale! Let's take it from the beginning. First off, you've got to admire, yet again, my breathtaking sense of location. My feel for environment. You can just see Arabia out there, shimmering in the sands. But Strange, as usual, is bored by his exotic surroundings. He's dealt with Farouk-al-Fauzi customs on more than a few occasions. He's stayed at the Dervish. He knows what a whirlpool is. He knows how to consume gallons of orange juice.

And later on just look at how I handle Strange at parties. Is this the *corps diplomatique* or what? The man's sense of style and *savoir-faire* is awesome. Greeting King Fauzi with the words, 'Your Highness … what a magnificent reception. Le tout Bahrain est ici,' has got to go down as one of the great openers. Too bad if Fuzz Nutz Fauzi hasn't a clue what he's on about, Strange has *got him in his power*, and from that point onwards the action are kept up remorselessly. The Mini-Moke. The phone booth in the desert. The rendezvous (French again) with the Sikorsky. The deal. The payoff. Fauzi buys it. Success City. Buzz is boggle eyed with admiration. And Strange? Well, Strange just proves he's a hell of a regular dude — 'one of the boys' — when he lays it on the line about having a *proper* drink. What a guy!

So there it is. I'm proud of *The Well-Notched Beretta*. It's a masterpiece. When you write *your* thriller just bear in mind the lessons I've taught you and you can't go wrong. You'll be besieged by publishers and agents clamouring for more. They won't be able to get enough of you. They'll want to shower you with $s and praise and %s. Which leads me on to the next and final section.

Dealing With Success

To many, success is a nebulous concept. Not to me. And I would like to think that all graduates of my writing school share my 'write-on' attitude to dealing with it. Success for me means cash, artistic recognition as one of the twentieth century's greatest writers and thinkers, twelve beautiful homes in twelve beautiful countries, waited on hand and foot by the kind of beauties I could only dream about before I put pen to paper for profit. And I won't even mention the yachts. But the hard shoulder of the highway to success is littered with the burnt-out shells of the fast-lane losers who couldn't make it.

So, take a tip from me: don't let it go to your head. Remember, you're only as good as your last review, only as good as your last bestseller. So when you read, 'This is not a book to be picked up lightly, it is to be hurled with great force,' in the *Tallahassee Town Crier* you know your work might just have hit a reef. Equally, when your publisher has remaindered your book before it's even published, you should be aware that all is not going to plan. But those are extreme examples. Mostly it's onward and upward in this game.

Don't get involved with all the shysters, bimbos, groupies, con-men and other lowlifers who are going to descend on you in the publishing world. Leave them to your agent: a big person in the life of a successful writer, but also someone to be put firmly in their place. Agents want minimum 10%. 10% of *your* earnings. 10% of *your* life. Sol Scirocco, my New York agent, approached me – in Vegas as I recall – after my massive success with *The Girl From Waco*. His standard % was 10. I said, 'Sol, it's gotta be 5, and as of this moment I have 100% of your life, 24 hours a day, and you have 5% of mine. Period.' I have to hand it to Sol, he was shrewd enough to see that 5% of me was a whole lot better than 10% of some dog who walked in off the street toting a dictionary, a sheaf of A4 and a half-spent biro. Sol is now a very rich man, but – as you'll have already guessed – I'm 95% richer than him. And that's the way I like it. So I say, take care of the percentages and the writing will take care of itself.

What more can I say? I've given you all the tips, all the insights, all the wisdom at my disposal on this great game we call writing. Success City beckons to you as a writer. Go live there.

In the dark days following the 1987 Stock Market crash, one man held a candle of hope. His book, The Impoverished Yuppie Survival Guide, *hit No. 1 on the bestseller list and stayed there month after month. To say it was a beacon for a million cruelly shattered Yuppie lives is to understate its significance. That man was Phil O. Facks. This book is his bible.*

The Impoverished Yuppie Survival Guide
by Phil O. Facks

It wasn't easy for you to seek out this information, because no matter what you may be pretending to your friends, purchasing *The Impoverished Yuppie Survival Guide* is an admission of hard times.

Society has us believe that the words 'impoverished' and 'Yuppie' are mutually exclusive terms. Don't believe a word of it. There are literally tens of thousands of people who, like you, for one reason or another, find themselves down on their luck, and unable to maintain that luxury fast-lane Yuppie lifestyle.

The global stock market crash of October 1987, improved procedures against insider trading, the massive drop in urban property values and a much higher success rate for cocaine possession convictions – there are a multitude of good reasons behind these many personal tragedies.

You may never work in an investment bank again, but with this guide you can lead a convincing and – above all – *affordable* Yuppie lifestyle which, teasingly, will leave what friends you have left wondering where the hell the money comes from.

Let's examine the essentials.

Cocaine
The quintessential Yuppie commodity and as a result very expensive. And definitely right out of bounds as far as your shopping list is concerned.

104

But, luckily for you, salt, washing powder and saltpetre remain relatively inexpensive items and, if you're careful, within reach of your domestic budget. So, by concealing its true identity, you can cut it along with the best of them. Anyway, since when did a gramme of Lux up the nose do anyone any harm?

The Porsche
Owning this motor is central to the Yuppie dream, and seeing it go was sheer trauma.

But don't despair. Those market-conscious West Germans have gone over to mass production of lifesize pedal-car Porsches! Made from krypton fibreglass, these light sporty roadsters come in all the classic Porsche colours, and are indistinguishable from the real thing!

Whether you risk being seen pedalling round the Hamptons or Knightsbridge is optional. But if you do the survival guide counsels disguised tinted glass; you don't want to be seen being wasted off the lights by Ford Pintos or Sinclair C5s.

The best advice would be to merely park the pedal-Porsche outside your current place of abode and be seen around it.

Video
If life without video is somehow a life lived incompletely, life with a secondhand b & w 1960s Ferguson, incommunicado with Channel 4, is a Yuppie hades.

But *film noir* is big news and there's a wave of 60s period nostalgia going down. And your Ferguson provides just that. Go for it.

Nightclubbing
No way are you now going nightclubbing (or dayclubbing). And the last thing you want is to be seen pathetically hanging round Stringfellows or the Limelight hoping for a posse of your old circle to take you in. They won't: they hate you now because you're poor.

Sounds
Out went the CD player and other top flight hi-fi accessories within days of your fall from grace, together with the compacts, albums and cassettes. What to do?

There's only one thing for it: a radio. Could this be the time to daringly reintroduce the 1950s concept of 'radio on' party entertaining? Yes, it could. Yes, it's going to have to be! But one bit of advice: don't dance to news broadcasts. It's unnatural.

Designer clothes

Those halcyon days strolling round trendy shops, spending more than four figures in less than $\frac{1}{2}$ an hour, suddenly seem remote as you face the financial reality of K Mart bin-end Romperettes for bus-E-ness ladies, flared Wave-E-Line sta-prest suit and a pair of different-sized, right-footed, 'El Gran Señor' naughahide shoes nicked from the local shoe shop display.

My solution to this problem is brilliantly simple. Tear out the invitation below, and carry it with you at all times.

Mr Ralph Lauren
Invites

. . . .

To a 'Classic Bad Taste' Party
At the Sherry Netherland Hotel,
New York City

RSVP

Armed with this invitation you can go anyplace, anytime. Think of it as your passport to Yuppie City.

The Filofax

Let's face it, the Filofax is the *sine qua non* of Yuppiedom. By now it's more than likely you've had to pawn your Cartier crocodile-skin 'fax. But if you're not prepared to get back into the ring with some type of 'fax then, in my view, you're not prepared to get into the ring at all.

Here's how you do it. Take the back of a Cornflakes packet, a piece of string, a wodge of betting slips you can find in any bookmakers, and a pot of glue. Then get an old *Blue Peter Annual*, which should give you more practical help than I can.

Culture

In all truth this was never a crucial item on the Yuppie shopping list, coming a poor 18th after Porsche shades. But it *was* on the list. Perhaps now's the time for *Das Kultur*. The big beef-up on twentieth-century painting? The ultimate reading challenge of *Brave New World*? Or a nightschool course on obscure East European films? I leave it to you.

The Dole Queue

This is definitely an unyuppie environment, and there's no escaping the fact it's going to be a big challenge. The Survival Guide counsels an elaborate disguise for your fortnightly visit.

Shrinks

Confessors to a million materialist dreams, shrinks are the unsung heroes of the Yuppie experience. How tragic your sessions should be brutally cut short just when you'd reached your childhood relationship with your mother after she refused to buy you a Ferrari. But no money = no shrink.

Don't panic. The new buzzword in psychotherapy is self-analysis, where you, the patient, lie down on the couch (or floor in your case, since you sold your furniture) and ask yourself searching questions. Read all about it in Dale Hendorsen's bestselling book *One Way Therapy* — which is an awful lot cheaper than employing a shrink — and eventually a lot more satisfying.

Food and Drink

Nipping out to the delicatessen for the odd bottle of Krug and rare French cheese is out of the question these days.

But never forget that *style is all* in the food and drink game. And just as with fashion, there are a thousand trendy food tribes out there, experimenting with wacky diets, pretending that Nigerian cheese prolongs your life by 300 years, etc. etc. Dire financial straits force you to join this bunch of wackos, and so, naturally, you find yourself on the 'Hermann J. Bendytoye Diet' — cabbage leaves and tap water, three times a day, 365 days a year. Daringly original, impressively severe and extremely cheap. Go for it.

Designer Exercising

Your membership at the exclusive gymnasium is a thing of the past, along with the Nautilus equipment and Dancin' Arnie Schwarzennegar training pumps. Now fitness for you means parks and public swimming pools; it means early morning runs along polluted streets; it means cleaning dog shit off your shoes. But fitness isn't something you can buy off the shelf, despite what they tell you. Fitness doesn't come by wearing Dancin' Arnies. It comes from hard physical effort. I want to see you go for it.

And if you have the embarrassing experience of bumping into a friend when jogging round some park in the centre of the city, explain you are very close to signing a development deal on the whole property, and that you are doing some 'on site' research.

Magazines and newspapers

Interiors, *Blitz*, *Elle* and *Vogue* are just some of the magazines which are essential components of the Yuppie home. Unfortunately they're very much on the pricey side for your pocket. Keep a weather eye open for the contents of garbage cans, or loiter round waiting rooms, enabling you, perhaps, to pick up a recent edition for free.

With newspapers the problem is less grave, as even you should have enough pennies to rub together to buy the *Independent* once a week, and then tote it round for the next six days. I don't have to tell you to conceal the date of the edition, do I?

Travel

Whether for business or pleasure, travel is a major part of the Yuppie dream — locations like Phuket, Mauritius, Klosters, The Village, Tokyo, and Virgin Gorda tripping all too easily off the tongue. It is, in fact, *an obligation* of the Yuppie to exude a cosmopolitan air.

Unfortunately the only travelling you'll be doing will be to the Job Centre. The solution is simple. At the library you can freely digest a range of travel books, and beef up on your general knowledge. But, beyond this, it's essential to cultivate an in-depth competence on obscure places, enabling you to hold forth on the suburbs of Tokyo, the lack of delicatessens in Baden-Baden, exactly why bus fares are so expensive in Quito, and how you and Tom Wolfe 'discovered' the Pez Dorado on Second and 116th Street.

Crime

Officially a very unyuppie activity. Unofficially it's the name of the game down on the trading floors. But you're no longer in the financial big league — remember? And although criminal activity and pecuniary advancement appeal to you, no Yuppie ever thought it was fashionable going into banks wearing a stocking over the face. Besides, crime equals the hideous possibility of prison — definitely the most unyuppie environment of all.

Stay clear of this activity.

So there you have it. *The Impoverished Yuppie Survival Guide* is the only handbook of its kind that deals with this problem — a problem that is going to loom larger and larger in the future. And if you think I'm wrong, only reflect that that man or woman in a Porsche today could be busking the underground or working the streets tomorrow.

The tailor at the cutting edge of style, that continental wizard Guy Perrière, is the man who has all the answers when it comes to what's in and what's out on the style scene. Way back in '75 I disregarded his advice on getting into widely flared trousers and was paying the social consequences for years afterwards. You don't make mistakes like that twice. If you're lucky — and pay attention to what he says here — you'll never make them at all.

The Style Formula
by Guy Perrière

My name's Guy Perrière. They call me the 'style guru'. If people want to know what material possessions are in on the style scene — and what are out — they come to me. And I advise them.

Now I'm advising you, the reader, what *crucial* possessions must be yours if you are to keep your place in smart society.

Let's face it, with manufacturers pandering to every conceivable whim, today's consumer has a bewildering assortment to choose from, and no one can blame you for a few rash purchase mistakes, a few errors of judgement. We've all made them, including myself: you'll be amazed to know I once bought a Rolls-Royce! Well, you live and you learn, as they say.

I want you to think of Guy Perrière's Style Formula as a friend. A friend who escorts you carefully through the maze of materialism to those essentials that you and your lifestyle require. Soon you will be the proud owner of stylish and beautiful possessions, and be envied by the less privileged, who think style is something you use to climb over hedges.

Let's introduce ourselves to that most potent status symbol of all:

Your Car
Style Formula Choice: *The Lada*
Glasnost and *perestroika* are more than just buzzwords. They stand for a swinging East European lifestyle that is fast becoming

the envy of the West. And no object encapsulates this more than the Lada.

The image is racy, with the accent on speed, while the design is strictly non-utilitarian. Recent models boast four-gear shifts, optional 'vanity' mirrors, optional ashtray and cigarette lighter, optional single-frequency car radio, and in their efforts to pander to Western luxuries, the Soviets have tossed in optional nylon carpets *throughout* the vehicle.

Ease yourself into the padded Glinka driving seat, hear the satisfying roar of that two-cylinder Gromyko engine, and know for sure that you are at the controls of one of Europe's most dynamic vehicles.

To a whole generation of Russians the Lada whispered of weekending in Kharkov; bring-a-potato parties; queue-jumping at Gum. And in the West the car exudes that same sense of stylish mystique, conferring upon the owner the distinction of being 'different'.

Your Business Accessories

Style Formula Choice: *The Scottcade Executive Briefcase*
Business is business, the world is saying, and young men and women everywhere are responding to its call. No stylish individual can, however, contemplate success in the world of commerce without a briefcase. And from an enormous variety available, there is only one which has a legendary, almost totemic, power: the Scottcade 'Executive'.

Cleverly, Scottcade haven't changed the design one iota since the heady days of June 1979 when this absolute classic first rolled off the production line. Even today its 100% genuine leather-style Kidron shouts 'authenticity' while its restricted contours make for an ideal lightweight travelling companion.

With the 'Executive' Scottcade pioneered the daring concept of combination locks, and there they are still — sitting smugly either side of the naughahyde handle. Flicking back the hinges with a metallic 'thunk' and opening the briefcase to reveal the sumptuous interior remains, to this day, a deeply satisfying experience. And as the back panel rests primly on its two cantilevered support brackets, the fantastic skill and vision of

Scottcade's original design team are laid bare: even now one is *amazed* by the sheer brilliance of the twin biro nozzle holders and plastic sectional dividers.

Going places in life? Make sure the 'Executive' is going with you.

Your Jewellery
Style Formula Choice: *The Waco ID Bracelet*
The twentieth century was gearing itself up to trample on and submerge the individual when, in 1911, Charles Waco forged his classic ID bracelet. Waco — a big forthright lathe worker from Miscogee — recognized the need for personal identity that lies in the heart of each and every man. His invention, a robust, stylized personal statement, was an immediate success with those wishing to distinguish themselves from the herd, and remains so to this day.

When selecting a Waco there is, inevitably, a wide range of metals to choose from. If cash isn't an issue, punters often go for the stylish platinum model with Christian name diamond inlay (*Donny*, see your name in lights!) or you can plump for the baser gold or silver. Whatever the metal, the classic lines of Waco's original ID are faithfully represented, and his instruction that each and every chain be sufficiently loose to prominently display your name on your hand is never deviated from.

Your Bathroom
Style Formula Choice: *The 'Sun King' Jacuzzi*
Since the days of Louis XIV, no single potentate has equalled the splendour and magnificence of Versailles, and in the world of bathroom plumbing no one has matched the unrestrained luxury and elegance of the 'Sun King' Jacuzzi — an absolute must for today's discerning hedonist with an eye for Style with a capital S.

The team that built the 'Sun King' in 1980 went back to Versailles for inspiration, and they found it in Le Nôtre's baroque triumph — the beautiful, scalloped, central fountain. And many of the 'Sun King's' most distinctive features have been lifted directly from it — the twelve partially submerged ring seats, the central raised dais and throne, behind which jets of water play, and ornate classical figurines in the frieze running round the inside circumference.

Made entirely from black marbled plastic, the 'Sun King' is further distinguished by solid gold taplets and – sophistications unknown in Louis' day – underwater video and alcove minibars.

Clearly the 'Sun King' is tailor made for social occasions and lucky owners tell of smart 'come as you are' jacuzzi parties with twelve guests seated around the host's central throne – a veritable Sun King (or Queen!) surrounded by stars in your solar system.

Practical Style
Style Formula Choice: *The Swiss Army Penknife*
Years on from making their first purchase, owners of this prestigious élite penknife still talk with excitement about the thrill when they feel its comforting shape in their pocket, or catch a glimpse of its sturdy attractive contours nestling next to the compact case in their handbag.

Even in these lawless days with personal safety at a premium, sporting a Bowie knife is considered a little 'gauche'. Much better, then, to plump for this stylish and practical penknife that has given the Swiss Army such a lethal reputation. For this is no ordinary weapon, and beneath its stunningly simple red cover lies an arsenal of instruments capable of terrible damage. In Swiss Army circles they still talk of the young teetotaller lieutenant who, trapped in the snow, held off a whole pack of cognac-laden St Bernards with his knife's nail scissors. While more recently, outside Saks Fifth Avenue, an independent young woman gutted her would-be mugger with her corkscrew.

For this is one fashion accessory that says, 'Don't tangle with me. I'm serious.' Combined with its classic good looks and devil-may-care conformity, it makes for the ideal bodyguard.

The World of Communications
Style Formula Choice: *The Carphone*
The carphone is Serious Style with a double S. It bellows 'I've arrived'.

113

But when you make your first purchase, it's essential that you buy a real one. Obvious as this may sound, a surprising number of inadequate show-offs are driving around having pretend conversations using toy phones, and the last thing you want for your fabulous new profile is to be associated with these people.

So. You're speeding down the M4 corridor in the Toyota Celica, listening to Richard Clayderman. The phone rings. It's your partner. Did you feed the cat? Did you renew the *Reader's Digest* subscription? Have you bought the dips for tonight's Tupperware party? Suddenly it's a domestic fracas.

Purely by conducting a conversation you will now be attracting admiring glances from less privileged fellow motorists, and it is at this juncture, just when it's getting ugly, that maximum cool is called for. Behave as if this was a bargaining session with your New York broker. Tough it out. Negotiate more cheese dips. Screw the *Digest*. We're talking image here, and with a carphone you've got one. So don't blow it. Look the part. Play the part.

Fashion Accessories
Style Formula Choice: *Tesco Shades*

The 1980s have seen the rise of an important fashion accessory for those seeking to advertise a stylish and elusive image: shades. But with the 90s fast approaching and other style statements — bones through noses, goatee beards and silly hats — all competing fiercely for space on the face, the suspicion grows that these twin guardians of anonymity will only stay in the 'must have' bracket if they can boast something extra special. This can only come through brand naming.

As a result, it's been exciting to watch Tesco launch its new brand name shades. It's an absolute classic, and of all the models currently in the market, this is *the* one with real staying power, having already edged out Porsche and Ferrari shades into second and third positions respectively. When it came to designing this superb accessory, Tesco went for a straightforward approach. It's a rich playboy look, underlined by mirrored rather than tinted glass. On the left lens in big, uncompromising gold letters are recorded the letters TE, above the plastic arm covering the bridge of the nose the letter S, and on the right lens the letters CO.

One of the most attractive and ingenious features is that the word TESCO is luminous, therefore lighting up prominently at night as you stroll round the purlieus of Covent Garden, the Quartier Latin or other style centres.

So, the message is clear. If you're sticking with shades into the late 80s and 90s, stick with Tesco.

Your Living Room
Style Formula Choice: *The Xanadu Floating TV Wax Lamp*
TV wax lamps became box office in the early 70s, casting an eerie glow over many a suburban living room. But of all the models on the market, it is only the Xanadu which has demonstrated real staying power, and remains to this day a much-prized feature.

The basic design of the Xanadu differs little from the norm: a 1ft high jelly-filled rectangular glass jar with recessed light bulb nodule — which conveys heat to the substance above it. But there all similarities end, for Xanadu were the first to pioneer remote control light switches, enabling TV viewers to change channels and light up the lamp simultaneously. Neither were they content to use standard whale blubber jelly — too heavy a substance to provide the spectacular writhing effect they were looking for. Eventually they found it in Kenji, a material used by Japanese taxidermists — and the benefits are all too obvious to see. And rather than offer a limited range of coloured light bulbs, Xanadu boast a kaleidoscope of different colours with which to illuminate the lamp.

A Xanadu is a talking-point feature of any sitting room.

The World of Practical Culture
Style Formula Choice: *The 'Stratford' Shakespeare Drinks Cabinet*
Even in the late twentieth century Shakespeare retains enormous street credibility, and owning a set of the Complete Works speaks volumes about you.

But these days the Bard is largely seen, not read, and few

people will sacrifice a good evening's video for *Coriolanus* or *Twelfth Night*. Realizing the punters were looking for image rather than culture, the Stratford Furniture Company designed the Shakespeare Drinks Cabinet. The idea is brilliantly simple: standing 2ft 6ins high and constructed from finest beechwood, the 'Shakespeare' displays, in leather-style Kidron, the spines of the forty-three plays, sonnets and poems. Designed to look exactly like real shelves of books, no one will realize the true purpose of the cabinet until you depress the letter 'b' in the centrally located edition of *Love's Labours Lost*, whereupon the twin doors fly open revealing your stocks of Malibu, Crème de Menthe and Bailey's. For convenience, the cabinet is refrigerated and has adequate space for glasses and highball mixers.

Luxury Clothes
Style Formula Choice: *The Speider Endangered Species Fur Coat*
There's been loads of ecological nonsense recently about the protection of endangered species. But don't let that fool you: for the style-conscious woman-about-town, with more than a little *chutzpah*, nothing can beat a rare fur coat. And when you're talking fur coats you've got to be talking a Speider.

Speider's company slogan 'No animal is safe' says it all. From giant pandas to macaque monkeys, from ring-tailed lemurs to cheetahs and minks, this enterprising company will track them down, and after a complicated tanning process these creatures will no longer be gambolling around their natural habitat but be racked up in Harrods' fur department or be a feature of I. Magnin's mix 'n' match annual wildlife spring fashion show.

Speider's furs are warm and cuddly and make a lady feel like a lady.

So. There it is. You now know what you've got to have to be right up there with the winners in society. These possessions are going to enhance your life in ways you barely imagined before. People are going to envy you; thieves will be anxious to rob you. In short, you will be the cynosure of all eyes. Enjoy.

Professor Don Rosenkrantz needs very little introduction from me. Sitting like a benign spider at the centre of the webs of world culture and learning, he has been described, in one of his many articles in the New York Times *as perhaps the most intelligent man in the history of the world. Now read on . . .*

The Connoisseur Rosenkrantz Arts Alphabet Program (CRAAP)

by Don Rosenkrantz

Hi! I'm Professor Don Rosenkrantz, and I know more than you. A whole lot more. Just because that's true, don't go getting mad at me. Wise up. You want what I've got: the intellectual capacity of a ZX Spectrum, my natty collection of academic ties, and a dick that's slightly bigger than a rolled serviette. But be realistic: I'm hardly going to donate my dick in the interests of culture. Or my ties for that matter. What I'm donating is my knowledge: the most extensive knowledge of world culture ever assembled in a single mind. And this knowledge can be *yours* with my Connoisseur Rosenkrantz Arts Alphabet Program — CRAAP — the entrée into the world of the arts that you've been craving.

It works like this. Say some schmuck like you is out to dinner and some smartarse intellectual like me asks if you've seen *Manon des Sources,* and you reach for the ketchup, I'm going to be marking you down as a zero, right? Let's be absolutely frank with each other. You think Mickey Spillane wrote many of Shakespeare's plays. You need to be set straight on the world of culture. So straight you can amaze people with astonishing facts about the art world's most celebrated characters.

So, there you go. All I need is $5000 for my Starter CRAAP Pack, made payable to me:

Professor Don Rosenkrantz,
The CRAAP Corporation,
Pomposity,
FLA.

But before you reach for your quill pen and chequebook, here's a taster of what my CRAAP is all about, to whet your ignorant appetite.

Austen, Jane.	Nineteenth-century writer and feminist. Only one of her books, *Pride and Prejudice*, about the notorious slave trader William Wilberforce was ever rated as good enough to be filmed, but she left an indelible mark on society in other, more important ways. With William Morris she founded the company that would become Britain's biggest motor manufacturer, and later, when she turned her back on industry, she showed she retained the golden touch by striking oil near the town in Texas which still bears her name.
Bacon, Francis.	Did Francis Bacon exist? Controversy still rages about whether the many outstanding canvases attributed to this painter were really the work of William Shakespeare.
Capote, Truman 'Al'.	Terrorized the New York literary underworld for decades. The Capo di Capi of celebrity chat shows, he gunned down his rivals in cold blood in a notorious early morning shoot-out immortalized in *Breakfast at Tiffanys*. Believed to have been the mastermind

behind CBS's hit series *The Wheel of Fortune*, but never proven.

Dylan, Bob.
Singer, songwriter and poet Dylan also starred in the noted television series, *The Magic Roundabout*. Perhaps his most celebrated works are *Under Milk Wood* and.

Euripides.
Philosopher, playwright and pops composer who never really scaled the heights of achievement attained by his first hit, 'Zorba the Greek'.

Forster, E. M.
Scion of the famous brewing family, celebrated Edwardian travel writer and founder of the Consumers' Association, E. M. Forster dedicated much of his life to a campaign to bring foreign hotels up to acceptable standards. His most important books are considered to be *A Room With A View* and *Howard's End*, a biography of the hotelier, Howard Johnson.

Goya, Francisco.
A very big wheel in the Spanish cosmetics biz, Goya is also known for his surrealist paintings and even more surrealist lifestyle! A multi-talented businessman and artist, he also wrote the hit single, 'I Should Be So Lucky'.

Hemingway, Ernest.
Fisherman, big game hunter, bullfighter and principal dancer with the Ballet Rambert for many years between the Wars. A friend of T. S. Eliot, he was the original American Express Gold Card holder.

Iacocca, Lee. One of the twentieth century's greatest philosophers, statesmen and car salesmen.

Joyce, James. Self-taught Irish writer who may have reached the highest class had he mastered the basics of punctuation and grammar. Several attempts have been made to film his rumbustious novels of Irish life, the most successful of which was probably *Finnegans Rainbow*, starring Petula Clark.

Kirkegaard, Søren. A stern unbending nineteenth-century Danish pastor, who would be surprised to learn he is a buzzword at trendy dinner parties.

Lawrence, D. H. Part-time estate gardener, Arabist and writer. Famed for riding a motorbike naked across Saudi Arabia and inciting the shocked inhabitants to revolt. Wrote *Lady Chatterley's Lover*. Married German air ace Baron von Richthoven.

Marx, Harpo. Writer, philosopher and comedian whose textbook on playing the world's stock markets, *Das Kapital*, is still read by millions of aspiring moneymakers.

Nobel, Alfred. A wealthy Swedish professor, Nobel is the man who gives away the big, big prizes in the arts world. It works like this: academics and artists the world over assemble annually in the giant Nobeldrome in Stockholm for his ever popular 'Arts Bingo Contest'. The Prof. calls out the numbers, and the lucky prize-winners get to collect the coveted Nobel Prize, a two-week holiday in Lund.

O, Histoire d'.
French sensualist writer, who achieved prominence in *fin-de-siècle* Paris. Publications include *Du Côté de Chez Mimi, Les Bondages de Montmartre* and the autobiographical *Histoire d'O.* Arrested for indecent exposure in the left luggage room at the Gare du Nord. Died in 1915, in Flanders, while on active service with a mobile laundry unit.

Parker, Dorothy.
Wit, writer and chief hit lady of the New York 1920s literary circuit, Parker went on to manage the career of Elvis Presley and become the role model for a principal character in the puppet series *The Thunderbirds.*

Quincy, Thomas de.
Eighteenth-century acid freak and author of the cult *Confessions of an Opium Eater.* A slave to fashion, he pioneered the introduction of stack heels and loon trousers into Georgian England. Organized the first non-electric Glastonbury Festival.

Rubens, Jerry.
Painter and revolutionary who shot to prominence in the 1960s, as self-styled leader of the Big Bottom Liberation Movement. The 'BBLM' was successful in America — not surprisingly — but failed to make much impact in Europe.

Stein, Gertrude.
The most misunderstood writer of the twentieth century, since literally no one could understand her baffling phrases,

e.g. 'to meat you meet to please you'. Went on to write an incomprehensible wine critique, *The Grapes of Wrath*.

Trollope, Anthony. Inventor of the letter-box, and thereafter a celebrated man of letters. It was often said that this mutton-chopped, bespectacled novelist spent so much time writing that he never noticed the reprehensible behaviour of his wife, who bequeathed the family name to those who followed her example.

Unter, Den Linden. Big Nazi era pops composer, who orchestrated the backing vocals on Adolf Hitler's massive 1939–45 European Tour.

Van Dyke, Dick. Dutch painter widely admired for such works as *The Laughing Cavalier* and *I Love Lucy*. Also – and this fact will amaze your friends – a major importer of Havana cigars until they were declared illegal. Best known now, perhaps, as an early influence on his close relative, Van Gogh.

Wagner, Richard. Noted composer and star of the hit TV series *Hart to Hart*. Playing opposite his wife Cosima, he scandalized his home town, Bayreuth, by wearing flaxen-haired wigs and Viking helmets.

Xerox, Rankis. Early Greek philosopher, most noted for his theory of duplication – put very simply, the notion that there exists somewhere a perfect version of everything that may be seen on earth.

Ever since it was first written people have been trying to invent a machine that would prove this law, not once but twice in a row without breaking down. So far they have met only failure.

Yeats, W. B.   Organ-playing poet and TV evangelist who was spectacularly defrocked before a national prime-time audience.

Zwicz, Tomasz.   Celebrated Polish film director. Numerous international successes include *Soviet Tractor Quota, Return of the Soviet Tractor Quota* and *The Soviet Tractor Quota Strikes Back*. Wrote the scores for the musicals *Five Year Potato Queue*, and *Come Gdansking*.

So. I've given you a privileged glimpse of my incredible databank of cultural knowledge that is CRAAP, and I'm willing to bet you're already a wiser person than you were when you first glanced at this article. But not wise enough yet, I fear, to distinguish Don Johnson from Dr Johnson, Johnson & Johnson, Ben Jonson, Jeremiah Johnson and Lyndon Johnson, and which two of those characters have appeared in *Miami Vice*.

I'll advertise once more. The Starter CRAAP Pack for state-of-the-art-ignoramuses is yours for $5000. Send it now.

These days, Dale Hendorsen comes on like a confident version of Rambo. But it wasn't always that way. Dale's account of his struggle for self-respect, and his superb analysis of what can be done to achieve it, has put him on the Fortune *list of the twenty most wealthy men in America. Welcome aboard, Dale, and I hope as many people as possible will share in your invaluable advice.*

Don't Lie Down To Be Stood Up — Assert Yourself!

by Dale Hendorsen Jnr.

I'm Dale Hendorsen Jnr. Would you believe for thirty long years of my life I couldn't bring myself to say that? Would you believe that for thirty years I was a social doormat, something people wiped their shoes on?

I'm a country boy from Scottsbluff, Nebraska. Pa slaughtered livestock for paydirt. Ma was Nebraska's champion mud wrestler. I guess they were totally wild people. That is until Pa got locked into the steer pen on a one-way ticket to Hamburger City, and Ma bought it one night partnering Chesty Morgan in a tag team.

So there I was. Orphaned at 18. Deeply shy. And with only my clerical job at J. C. Penneys between me and a welfare check. I lived a troglodyte existence. I was virtually invisible. Except to dogs who confused me with lamp-posts. It was in the Fall of 78 that my life changed. I was in J. C.'s customer lift taking some dockets to Soft Toys, and wondering whether I could make it home to catch *The Price is Rite*, when the lift stops at Cosmetics and in walks this beautiful lady. I was stunned.

We were alone. Somewhere inside me a voice said, 'Kid, you've gotta make your move.' So I said, 'My name is Dale Hendorsen Jnr,' and she said, 'Shove it up your ass, blowmonkey.'

124

I didn't watch *The Price is Rite* that night. I thought long and hard about what happened. And I figured: OK. You've had a mega-rejection. But at least you made your move. *At least you tried to assert yourself.* And it felt good. So good I couldn't stop asserting myself. Within a month I was talking to strangers and waving at policemen. Girls became a part of my life. And I became a part of theirs. I told J.C.'s they could take their job and give it to some other sucker. I joined an insurance company selling policies. Within a year I had sold more lifers in the State of Nebraska than the company sold in a decade. I didn't take no for an answer, and my motto, 'Your money or your life', reinforced by a Magnum held to the head opened doors and cheque books everywhere.

But pretty soon I tired of that game. I knew what I had discovered about myself could be sold to people who suffered the trauma of unassertive lifestyles. So I went public. My first advertisement for the 'Don't Lie Down To Be Stood Up' Program in the *Scottsbluff Town Crier*, entitled 'Are You A Wimp?' drew only one response from a local pharmacist who committed suicide before I cashed his pledge cheque, so I figured: let's beef it up some. The next ad., headlined 'Do You Want To Blow Them ?' brought 16 responses, 14 of which were from middle-aged unmarried women, 2 from policemen.

The response had been encouraging, though I knew it needed refining. I believe it was my next advertisement which set the tone for my success story and became the clarion call for my whole assertiveness philosophy. 'Make My Day' was an immediate hit in Scottsbluff, bringing in literally hundreds of signatories for the Program and I used the same formula for statewide and ultimately national advertising.

So. Now you've parted with your initial down payment of $25,000 on the 'Don't Lie Down To Be Stood Up' Program, let's get down to business. Assertive business.

I like to hinge 'Don't Lie Down' around some realistic hypothetical situations.

Lesson A
Situation No. 1: AT THE BEACH
You're enjoying a day's relaxation at the beach, leafing idly

through the Sears Roebuck catalogue for some intellectual stimulation, when some very assertive individuals kick sand in your face, steal your costume and bury you in the shallows as the tide comes in. Though coastguards rescue you in the nick of time, it's hardly a good day for your self-esteem.

Let's look at the scene, using the 'Don't Lie Down' Method. You walk on to the beach to be met by the same tormentors.

Follow very carefully — and in sequence — my copybook advice for this situation.

1. Distract your adversaries by doing something unusual. Options include:

a) Singing Maurice Chevalier's Every Little Breeze seems to Whisper Louise in falsetto.

b) Picking up a handful of sand and eating it.

c) Serving a meal to imaginary guests around you.

and then . . .

2. Walk up to the ringleader and say, word for word: 'You come near me again and I'll sing Neil Sedaka'.

Unorthodox and eccentric, perhaps, but a fine way of asserting yourself and ensuring you can walk back to that beach with confidence any darn time you choose.

Situation No. 2: THE PARTY

I don't claim to be a mind-reader or a magician, but years of teaching assertiveness therapy have given me an ability to construct a profile of my readership with an accuracy quotient of no less than 98%. I know you, and I know you hate parties.

If you're a girl you're a permanent wallflower. You dread being invited to parties and you only show up because you're not assertive enough to turn down the invitation. You dress in the kind of dowdy clothes even Queen Victoria declined to wear. You get into a corner and you try to turn invisible. You keep your coat on because you don't dare to ask where to put it. You try not to speak to anyone and hate yourself for it. You envy more glamorous and interesting women. You go further than that: you loathe them. It's a long party and you're almost the last to leave because you didn't want to look like the first to go. And then everyone left in a bunch. Then you feel you have to offer to do the washing up. Then the only other person left at the party — a weird-looking creep with extra-thick glasses and a bizarre habit of picking his nose with both hands at once — suggests that you go back to his place for 'coffee'. By now you feel obliged to accept, and before long find yourself in the all-too-familiar position of being tied naked to a bed, while the boggling four-eyed lowlifer salivates in front of you. Will you ever learn to assert yourself?

If you're a guy, the situation is no better. You go to parties because you don't know any girls and every time you think that some beautiful chick might just walk up to you, and ask you to go to bed with her. You get to the party, and the chicks are there alright, but you're so scared you dive back into the kitchen for a glass of water and a three-hour perusal of last year's calendar hanging on the wall. Then you begin to worry that people are laughing at you — not without reason I should add. Then you run away, crying. You're going nowhere. Fast.

Let's look at one of the most central problems: your image. It's terrible. These days you are what you look. Splash out on some contemporary threads, and a pair of Ray-Bans.

With your image sorted, at the next party you go to try any of the following assertive actions:

a) Approach the most attractive member of the opposite sex you can see and say, 'I'd like to marry you.'

b) On entering the crowded room, scream at the top of your voice, 'The Prince of Darkness has arrived!' Then strip off down to a pair of black diamanté briefs.

c) Interrupt the liveliest conversation you hear and say, 'So *that's* what you think of French cheeses.'

Believe me, this way you'll have made an assertive impression on everyone.

Situation No. 3: AT WORK
The day you agreed to polish the senior Vice-President's Mercedes with your own clothes was the day you destroyed your career, and not even the most ardent optimist would claim your prospects in paperclip supplies department are rosy. The betting is you might get a desk, with three legs, by the time

you're fifty. That is if you play your cards right, and that could mean cleaning the entire executive limo fleet on a daily basis.

What went wrong? Easy answer: *they knew you could be pushed around*. They knew you'd perform any task, however demeaning. THEY KNEW YOU WEREN'T ASSERTIVE. Clearly, extreme measures are called for. ASSERTIVE MEASURES. And, as I see it, the following course of action is your only way out of the professional cul-de-sac in which you find yourself.

Try any of the following:

a) Barge unannounced into a main board meeting wearing a white gown and angel wings. Say you have come to save the company. The board will not be able to overlook your assertive, and well-meaning, intrusion.

b) Steal one of the VPs' suits and clean his Mercedes with it. The VP will be certain to see the joke in this, and word will get round about your assertive and fearless panache.

c) Torch the entire fleet. You won't have a job. But you will have asserted yourself.

OK, so there you go. But hey, let's get back to basics.

Improving Assertiveness through Negative Self-Flagellation

Deep down you think you're a failure. But don't be bashful. You *are* a failure: and it is only by recognizing this that you can break back into the world of successful assertive behaviour.

To do this you must first go through my 'Unassertive Acceptance' syndrome — meaning you *positively acknowledge* your inadequacy. Having touched bottom you can then fight your way back. Let's look at it.

You've got nothing to boast or show off about in life. So — don't boast. Level with yourself. Say you're at a party and some smartarse asks you what you do. Say you do nothing except play frisbee with your cat and listen to Leonard Cohen. Or say you're at an interview for a job and the boss asks you why you're qualified for the position. Level with him — say you're completely unqualified for it and it'd be catastrophic to appoint you. Finish the interview by bursting into tears.

Tough medicine — but it is only by recognizing the parameters of our inadequacy and unassertiveness that we can progress to being assertive human beings.

The Flight-or-Fight Syndrome

Don't lie down to be stood up. It sounds so easy, doesn't it? But it's hard for weak and inadequate people to rewrite history. A dog urinates on you. You want to bring it to heel. Small children insult you. You want to frighten them away. A taxi driver rips you off. You want to commit homicide. But you do none of these things. You fail to assert yourself. You're acting out the *Flight Syndrome*: an attitude of mind that does nothing for your self respect and everything for your 'opponents'.

It's tough out there. You've got to assert yourself. You must get into the *Fight Syndrome*.

Let's look at some complex, advanced situations to illustrate this.

Lesson B

Situation No. 1: REFUSING DOOR-TO-DOOR SALESMEN

A man knocks on your door offering a range of plastic furniture and Tupperware. You've already got the items in question. The salesman is persistent. You end up with two sets.

What went wrong? You caved in, that's what went wrong. It's the *Flight Syndrome*. You need the *Fight Syndrome*, and fast. So when some schmuck puts his foot in your door, you're not going to take that. Keep an axe handy, so if he gets pushy with you – like foot in the door pushy – you can get pushy with him. Like hacking his foot off pushy.

Lesson C

Situation No. 1: (a) ASKING FOR A PAY RISE

Never easy this one, but no assertive person ever laid claim to that title by earning peanuts. Try holding a loaded pistol to your boss's head until he starts talking the right numbers.

(b) DECLINING A PAY RISE

Every boss has to do this. A superb technique is to offer an unusually low chair to the applicant, and more importantly a chair that is constructed from imitation leather and makes a loud farting sound every time he/she moves.

Situation No 2: NOISY NEIGHBOURS
You've been kept awake by jive ass music from the neighbours. Give them one warning. But only one. Then you go in: through a window SAS style. Forcibly remove K-Tel albums, tossing a stun grenade behind you as you leave.

Situation No. 3: TAKING BAD FRUIT BACK TO THE GREENGROCERS
The greengrocer who sold you rotting lychees and avocados thought you were a pushover. How wrong could he be! Take the fruit back. Exchange it. Then force the greengrocer to eat the bad fruit at gunpoint, including the stones.

Learning to Say 'No'

People like you have difficulty saying 'no'. And this is sad, because as a result you are ruthlessly exploited by others. But it doesn't have to be this way: as in so many other things, attaining negative responsiveness is simply a matter of perseverance and training.

Let's look at some conversations setting what you might have said in response to a question or statement against what you will say after absorbing the *Dale Hendorsen Jnr method*. Set your hat at a jaunty angle and go for it!

Question/Statement	Unassertive Response	Assertive Response
Policeman: I'm booking you for visually assaulting an officer.	OK, I'm guilty.	You're beautiful when you're angry.
Boss: You're fired.	You've every right to be doing this to me.	You fire me, and I'll torch you and your office.

Question/Statement	Unassertive Response	Assertive Response
Mugger: Give me your money.	Would you like my house key as well?	I am a master of the 8th Dan. Desist, or you're catfood.
Hotel Desk Clerk: Your room's been taken. There's a cupboard by the lift shaft.	Thank you so much. I assume there's no room rate reduction.	I am a master of the 8th Dan. I have the Regal Suite or you're dogfood.
Employment Officer: We have a position as a lavatory cleaner. After three years you get a brush.	I'll take it, and don't worry about the brush.	Eat it raw, fuzznuts.
Bank Manager: Your current account is overdrawn by £2.60. This must be rectified immediately.	Please, I beg you, give me time.	You people are total parasites. I withdraw my account.
Date: I never want to see you again.	I'm sorry for being born.	The next time you see me will be at the altar.

To assert yourself in life is to live. To not assert yourself is to wither and die. It's as simple as that. Believe me, I know. No one is saying it's easy: if they do, correct them. Assertively. It's hard. *Don't Lie Down* couldn't stretch you more thoroughly. But you needed to be stretched. You'd sunk so low your self-esteem probably measured less than 1% on the Steinruther Confidence Scale. Drastic steps had to be taken. And you've taken them. Now you don't need to *Lie Down* or be *Stood Up* anymore. You can stand up with the best of them and *Make Your Day*.

When they come to write the history of twentieth-century finance, the stock market crashes of 1929 and 1987 will pale into insignificance beside the catastrophe that Milt N. Keynes IV predicted in his worldwide bestseller, Surviving the F.L.O.O.D. *I don't mind telling you that I have followed Milt's advice in protecting my investments, and have watched them mature in a most exciting and unusual way. It's not too late for you to climb aboard.*

Surviving the F.L.O.O.D.

by Milt N. Keynes IV

Noah was a wise man. He saw what was going to happen, and he prepared himself for calamity. No doubt, on that last torrential day, as the Ark lifted off, there were a lot of people — unsmart people, suddenly about to be very dead people — who were knocking frantically on his door. No doubt it was tough to leave them behind. No doubt he shed a tear or two. But, and this is a crucial but, everybody had had the opportunity to assess the global situation. Everybody had had their chance to get out. And it was only Noah who sailed away with his investments, his family of animals and his future intact.

My name is Milt N. Keynes IV. I'm World President of Milt N. Keynes Investments Incorporated, and I want to share with you my analysis of the impending catastrophe in the world's financial markets. A catastrophe so large, it's going to make 1929 and 1987 look like single showers in a long hot summer. A catastrophe so cataclysmic, that millions of people are going to be swept away. And just as God told Noah to build his Ark, I'm telling you how to construct your means of survival when the world's financial markets collapse around your ears. Follow my advice and you will survive. Tell all your friends about it, because like Noah, you don't want to be shedding tears as *your* Ark lifts off, and *they're* clamouring outside in the deluge.

So. What is the nature of this deluge that is about to engulf the world? This F.L.O.O.D.? As if you didn't already know, F.L.O.O.D. stands for Financial Loss Of Optimistic Dollars. It is the basis of my worldwide investment policy and the source of my entire financial philosophy. F.L.O.O.D. is coming. Soon. The last ten years have seen a boom in the United States and Western Europe, while the Asian economies have been growing ferociously. People have become incautious about their investments, and they've placed what I call 'Optimistic Dollars'. But, as the breakdown below quite clearly shows, the good times are over — even if the markets don't know it yet. A combination of several things, some of them too complex to explain here, but including, basically, the Chinese birthrate, the Taiwanese plastics explosion, the death of the Duke of Windsor, *glasnost*, *perestroika* and Pepsi-Cola, have come together to put an irreversible brake on industrial growth, and therefore to doom all conventional investments to a speedy death. The Age of Optimism is over. The Period of Pessimism is upon us. You'd better believe it.

Let's look at the key areas.

Stocks and Bonds

A little while ago the media was full of the so-called Stock Market 'Crash'. I was selling stocks for months before it happened, and buying them the day after. Now I'm selling again, and if you want to keep your children off the streets you'll do the same. Stocks are about to go into major free fall. Without a parachute. The only things I'm buying into at present are Valium, gas ovens and razor blades! But seriously, friends, you have been warned. What happens when all the Optimistic Dollars — the O.D.s — are lost in the plunge? The world will send for the Pessimistic Dollars — the P.D.s — and only a few people are going to have them. Seems simple, doesn't it? Well, try explaining it to the IMF!! I've been circulating my monthly newsletter, 'F.L.O.O.D. TIME', to those turkeys for ten years now and, believe me, either they can't read, or they don't know what's good for them. I say get your money out — fast.

Commodities

Oil The world is full of oil. Don't let anyone tell you otherwise. In the 1970s the so-called oil 'crisis' drove gas prices through the ceiling and nearly brought about the end of civilization as we knew it. And why? So that a bunch of Arabs in sheets and sunglasses could go to Keenland and buy every yearling in sight. Now don't get me wrong on this — King Fauzi II happens to be a personal friend of mine — but just whose word did we have for it that there wasn't any oil left? You got it. The people who owned the oil. My own researches, which include infra-red satellite pictures capable of delivering magnified scans of Fauzi's personal swimming pool, indicate that Bahrain alone is sitting on enough gas to power the whole world well into the 25th century. Now that's a long time. And when I go public on this story, Texaco stocks aren't going to be worth the paper they're written on. Get out, while the going is good.

Diamonds You may think that Sierra Leone is just another strife-torn African republic. Just another third world state with more than its just allotment of coups and economic problems.

That's all going to change. Only the other day I had a man to man chat with President Kinshasha, SL's strongman leader, during one of my whirlwind trips round Black Africa. And you know what he told me? The entire Bo-Bo mountain range, Leone's biggest high-rise land mass, had been discovered to be made entirely of diamond rock formations. OK, this electrifying disclosure came after 18 pints of Wildebeest Lager, so I figured I'd take this with a pinch of salt. But my scepticism was dispelled after meeting Finance Minister Ju-Ju Bafodia who let slip troops had been despatched to the Bo-Bos to seal off the area which, as of yesterday, like immediately, had become government property.

This set my mind working. After two number crunching hours my Tel-Star calculator, I concluded the discovery of 14 billion tons of virgin diamond reserves would devalue the world market by 17,110%, making this highly valued gem as worthless as a shard of broken glass. Needless to say I got out of diamonds immediately. Get out now. You may have only minutes to spare. *Gold* I say get out of it. *Now.* You say: 'What?!' And I repeat, without prevarication, get out of gold before your investments disappear like ice cubes in the Mojave desert.

But *why* exit from this valuable commodity, recognized since the beginning of time as one of earth's most prized metals? Why get out of a commodity which you've been led to believe is the mainstay of the world's economies? And there you have the answer: you've been 'led to believe' that gold is the 'numero uno' game to be in, the sure mainstay against a rainy day — and boy, is it going to be rainy!

It's all a lie. My research has revealed that global gold reserves were exhausted as long ago as 1912. A massive cover-up, orchestrated by financiers and mining companies has persuaded a gullible world otherwise. As you lovingly ease that 'gold' ring on to your loved one's finger at the wedding ceremony, just think how you'd be feeling if you knew, as I know, that that precious object is, in fact, made entirely from the basest pig-iron.

I'm going to blow the whole thing wide open. Very shortly. The guilty people are going to be exposed. And in the process the fake edifices of the gold markets are going to crack and crumble into dust. The message is clear. Sell, sell, sell.

Plastics For decades plastics were the sexiest game in town, in terms of inflation-guaranteed earning %s. Not any more. This is down to Taiwan, which has produced the greatest glut of plastics products the world has witnessed. The Taiwanese have gone, literally, plastics crazy. Do they seriously believe the world market can handle a 6 billion ton production of plastic cutlery per *month*? How long do they think parents are going to put up with their tacky toys? Do they *really* see plastic disposable knickers lifting off in Western markets? (Rubber yes, plastic no — and lifting *down* surely?)

The market is unstable. It's going to collapse. Don't hang around plastic any more.

Pulling your investments away from these dangerous, dangerous commodities and minerals was almost the smartest move you ever made. But there's one even smarter move to be made, so smart you'll be sinking your teeth into the classiest piece of investment action all points North, South, East and West of Wall

Street. I won't be coy: Milt N. Keynes Investments offer you wealth, happiness and financial peace of mind, enabling you to not just avoid the F.L.O.O.D., but to float away on it to live happily ever after. Just like Noah escorted his priceless investments from the animal kingdom on to the safety of his Ark, so I am going to give you the chance to join my unique 'two-by-two' new wave investment plan. The choice is plain, and the choice is yours. Either you sink or you swim. And just like Noah, I have only a limited amount of room in my investment scheme, so I urge you to join *now*, before the torrent sweeps you away.

O.K. Let's look at the principles behind the plan. I know what you're thinking: Milt N. Keynes has spent a lot of time telling us to get *out* of all the investments the world, in its ignorance, considers safe and profitable, and now he's telling us to get into something else. What's the story?

The story begins, as I've said before, with Noah. Why exactly did Noah fill up his Ark with two of everything? I've got no wish to offend my family readership, but the implication is clear: they were there to *procreate* — so that they could populate the world when the flood receded. My unique 'two-by-two' policy is built along the same lines. I nominate *pairs* of investment opportunities which will survive into the new age. Individually, they are useless. Taken together, they generate the kind of wealth that will enable survivors to dominate the world economy for millennia to come from penthouse apartments, recently vacated by suicidal bankers and moguls swept away in the deluge as F.L.O.O.D. hit town. In the business world we call this synergy.

The Milt N. Keynes Space Mining Investment Corporation

Ark Twin Investment No. 1. 'The resource'. Why is Uranus called Uranus? Because it's made of uranium, dummy! I know, because I've been there. Two years ago I commanded an interplanetary probe to prospect the planet. Uranus is Uranium City, and despite what you read the world is going to need a whole lot more of that stuff. Forget Gorby, Friends of the Earth and the Peace Corps, uranium is here to stay and is going to be a big

big investment for decades to come. Needless to say, I have the exclusive mining rights to the planet in question for perpetuity.

For every dollar invested I am guaranteeing you a return on capital of 11,117% – *but only if you twin your investment.*

Ark Twin Investment No. 2. 'Transport facilities.' The incredible deposits of uranium at my disposal on Uranus are useless unless we can transport the product back to Earth. That's where the Milt N. Keynes Trans-Ur-Anus fleet of hi-speed space trains come in. They're in a siding at Milwaukee Central Station just waiting for the word. *Your* word. *Your* dollars. I want them. You've got them. Let's get moving.

Milt N. Keynes Third World Investment Opportunities

Ark Twin Investment No. 1. 'The product.' I've had loads of money tied up in one of the Third World's most successful and promising companies for more years than you've had hot dinners. Very few people have heard of Muhamor Radios, Hyderabad, and that's just the way I like it. Believe me, this company's sales graph looks like the Himalayas – up, up and up.

Ark Twin Investment No. 2. 'The marketing tie-in.' My investment in Muhamor's would be worthless if it wasn't twinned in a totally binding way with another thrusting Indian company raking in the rupees – the Sub-Continent Contraceptive Co. Everyone knows that the Indian government is giving away free radios for frequent and plentiful use of contraceptives, but only a handful of people have been in on Muhamor's and Sub-Continent Contros belonging to the same group! The government may be giving these items away free; but they're not *getting* them for free!! No, sir.

Taken together, this is a once in a lifetime opportunity. Grasp it now.

Milt N. Keynes Real Estate Investment Opportunities

Ark Twin Investment No. 1. When F.L.O.O.D. hits town, and some very, very rich people are suddenly very, very poor, they'll

137

be desperate to get at some liquid cash. And that means big, big opportunities to purchase their penthouses and palaces for derisory sums. And I mean *derisory*.

When F.L.O.O.D. hits town, we're going to be there making successful bids for prestige properties, laying down the kind of money you'd take to go shopping at K-Mart.

Ark Twin Investment No. 2. Now get this. Hordes of poverty stricken will be streaming out of their luxury residences in Manhattan, Florida, the Hamptons, etc; and apart from being recently poor, they'll have something else in common. They'll be recently homeless.

That's where we come in. Not only is Milt N. Keynes going to purchase their exclusive homes for peanuts, he's going to have a big slice of the action when it comes to resettlement. They're desperate, right? And desperate people will do desperate things. Like buying a plot of swampland in the Everglades, for 1000% more than it cost me in the first place. Or cost you, rather.

So, with *Ark Twin Investment No. 1* we're talking bottom dollar prices for top dollar real estate. And with *Ark Twin Investment No. 2* we're talking top dollar prices for shit. That makes sense in my book, and unless you're crazy it'll make sense in yours.

But, in order to get your hands on a portfolio of exclusive properties we're talking upfront investments. Nothing huge. Nothing excessive. Each share in the Milt N. Keynes Investment Opportunity Trust is valued at $125,000. The minimum stake is 100 shares per investor. A bit of a shell-out in the pre-F.L.O.O.D. phase, but worth each and every goddam' cent later on. Believe me. Trust my Trust.

The Milt N. Keynes Sub-Aqua Timeshare Experience

Fancy a place that's quiet, a little offbeat? Somewhere R & R really means just that: rest and relaxation, away from the nightmare of modern living? Welcome to the Milt N. Keynes Sub-Aqua Timeshare Experience.

Just off Key Biscayne, Florida, the village-style development will feature luxury apartments, quaint shopping streets, gourmet restaurants (seafood a specialty) and sizzling, sizzling nite spots. And all of it a mile underwater. Just think of it: no crowds of tourists with enormous asses, no gaudy souvenir hawkers, no dangerous traffic problems, no cancer-inducing suntans. The Milt N. Keynes Sub-Aqua Timeshare Experience has nothing to offer ... except the tranquillity and exclusivity that a truly great underwater holiday can provide.

How does it work? Basically, a sub-aqua timeshare is like any other timeshare agreement: you buy your apartment for a week – or for as many weeks as you like – and return to it at the same time each year. The big difference between the Milt N. Keynes Sub-Aqua Timeshare Experience and other, land-based time-shares, is that while the others are basically just holiday homes, the sub-aqua development is a major, distinctive, investment opportunity not to be missed. Just think about it. On land, you have bad weather, droughts, plagues and people who say, 'Have a nice day.' You have fires, earthquakes and other disasters both personal and natural. It's a known fact that 99.99% of all heart attacks and related illnesses happen above sea level, and what about the constant threat of nuclear war? Make no mistake: underwater is the living environment of the future. To build your own apartment on the sea bed would cost you millions of dollars. To buy into this project, with the introductory offer detailed below, is a proven opportunity that anyone can afford. Let's get down and boogie in an aquamarine world.

Ark Twin Investment No. 1. I am asking you to buy into this underwater dreamworld of mine. The investment per apartment per week is going to cost you $220,000. And that is $220,000 on the table right now, please. Thank you.

Ark Twin Investment No. 2. Now hear this. Each timeshare comes with exclusive rights to fish outside your apartment. And the rights come free. Now don't think that I've just chucked this in to sweeten the investment equation. The ocean off Key Biscayne is home to the Silver Fluted Carp – one of the most prized and valuable fish in the global aquarium. When you go fishing underwater off Key Biscayne, you go fishing for the big bucks.

Yes, I want to part with the huge sum of $220,000 to Milt N. Keynes Sub-Aqua Timeshares Incorporated, in exchange for a week's timeshare in a sub-aqua apartment.
I recognize that I am totally insane.
Signed:

So. There you go. I've shown you a few of the amazing two-by-two investments that fill up my Ark. I want to see you walking up the gangplank. I want you on board.

Noah's Ark floated off millions of years ago, but the human race hasn't learned much from that catastrophe, has it? Who says it'll be different when F.L.O.O.D. comes? Heed my words of wisdom, my 'Genesis' of the financial world, before you're swept away. Join me now.